"*Keeping Place* is a lovely reflection on home—from our spiritual longing to the nitty gritty of keeping a house. As Jen takes us through reflections on her life and other people's stories, through literature and Scripture, I was grateful to delve deeper into the role of place in many aspects of our lives. In a transient time, this book is a welcome invitation to consider how we do life with each other and with God."

Kent Annan, author of *Slow Kingdom Coming* and *Following Jesus Through the Eye of the Needle*

"Jen Pollock Michel takes us through the Scriptures as she explores the stories of God's people displaced, wandering, and longing for home. She captures the tension in all of our hearts: we are longing for something more, something permanent, and something better. We are longing for home—a place. Jen gently encourages us, reminding us that though we are longing, God has given us a home to tend to, people to love and care for, and a table for feasting and sharing. Ultimately, she points us to the only one who can fulfill our every longing—Jesus. Our home is in and with Christ, and one day we will be with him forevermore. Until then, Jen helps us learn to keep place."

Trillia Newbell, author of *Enjoy* and *Fear and Faith*

"With her signature depth and grace, Jen Pollock Michel casts a vision of home as both a human desire and a heavenly promise. She calls us to build imperfect dwellings alongside our loved ones in this life precisely because we are destined for a perfect dwelling in the life to come. Women and men alike will find joy in her vision of keeping house. This is a book that invites you in and lets you stay awhile, and I'm grateful for it."

Katelyn Beaty, former managing editor, *Christianity Today*

"It is one thing to write truth, and another to write it beautifully. With the skilled and hypnotic prose I have come to eagerly expect of her, Jen Michel invites us to consider the sacred space of home and the sacred duty of its keeping. We are seekers of home by design, and our homesickness is no accident. Exploring the rhythms of plenty and loss, worship and work, routine and rest, Michel exhorts us, male and female, to be faithful homemakers until such time as we inhabit our true and final dwelling place. In a time when transience and individuality mark the lives of many, she offers here a worthy meditation for the people of God."

Jen Wilkin, author of *None Like Him*

"Jen Pollock Michel has a unique gift of making theology come alive. She weaves a rich knowledge of scripture with her own compelling story, offering us a fresh perspective of a God who is the maker and keeper of place, the creator who cultivates the space where we find ourselves and the eternal home we long for. Her perspective is original, fresh, and unexpected."

Micha Boyett, author of *Found*

"What an amazing book this is! Jen Pollock Michel takes us on a journey through Scripture, church history, and the many places she has called home as she paints a picture of God as the ultimate Homemaker. *Keeping Place* stirs and prods us to consider our contributions to establishing a sense of home in today's world, even as we ache with homesickness for the New Jerusalem God has promised."

Trevin Wax, managing editor, The Gospel Project, author of *Counterfeit Gospels*

"Rife with scriptural acuity and sumptuous prose, *Keeping Place* has become my favorite read of the year. Michel's command of both tradition and the hunger of our age is at once refreshing and comforting. She invites us to embrace the shadow of something more that lingers at the edge of hearts, elucidating how the journey homeward happens only together with those here now and those gone before. *Keeping Place* rivals and bests most contemporary meditations on desiring the kingdom, and Michel has continued in this second book a trajectory of some of the finest scriptural grounding and pastoral care in print today."

Preston Yancey, author of *Out of the House of Bread*

KEEPING
PLCE

Reflections on the Meaning of Home

JEN POLLOCK MICHEL

FOREWORD BY SCOTT SAULS

IVP Books

An imprint of InterVarsity Press
Downers Grove, Illinois

InterVarsity Press
P.O. Box 1400, Downers Grove, IL 60515-1426
ivpress.com
email@ivpress.com

InterVarsity Press® is the book-publishing division of InterVarsity Christian Fellowship/USA®, a movement
of students and faculty active on campus at hundreds of universities, colleges, and schools of nursing in the
United States of America, and a member movement of the International Fellowship of Evangelical
Students. For information about local and regional activities, visit intervarsity.org.

Scripture quotations, unless otherwise noted, are from The Holy Bible, English Standard Version,
copyright © 2001 by Crossway Bibles, a division of Good News Publishers. Used by permission. All rights
reserved.

While any stories in this book are true, some names and identifying information may have been changed
to protect the privacy of individuals. All addresses in this book have been fictionalized.

"Genesis 15" in chapter eight is used by permission of Laura Merzig Fabrycky.

"Still Life" in chapter ten is used by permission of Wipf & Stock Publishers.

Cover design: Cindy Kiple
Interior design: Daniel van Loon
Images: yellow wooden background: ©narloch-liberra/iStockphoto
        door knocker: ©Bernard Van Berg/EyeEm/Getty Images

ISBN 978-0-8308-4490-6 (print)
ISBN 978-0-8308-9224-2 (digital)

Printed in the United States of America ∞

Library of Congress Cataloging-in-Publication Data
A catalog record for this book is available from the Library of Congress.

P	18	17	16	15	14	13	12	11	10	9	8	7	6	5	4	3	2	1
Y	32	31	30	29	28	27	26	25	24	23	22	21	20	19	18	17		

To my husband, Ryan:
Having and holding you is my joy.

To my mother, Jan:
Your love bears all things.

Thank you.

If I had one particular complaint, it was that my life seemed composed entirely of expectation. I expected—an arrival, an explanation, an apology.

MARILYNNE ROBINSON, *HOUSEKEEPING*

CONTENTS

FOREWORD

Scott Sauls

I AM CURRENTLY IN MY FORTIES and yet have never been fully or finally at home.

Throughout our childhood, Mom and Dad moved us to a new city every two years because of corporate job transfers. Childhood was followed by four years of college, six months teaching tennis in Kentucky, a three-month hiatus in Atlanta, and three-and-a-half years in Saint Louis for seminary. After that, we spent twelve years planting two churches in two different states, followed by five years in New York City and, to date, almost five years in Nashville.

My wife, Patti, and I swear that we are never leaving Nashville. We are in full agreement, the two of us are, that we are finally *home*.

But are we?

We also swore, early on, that we would give more lasting roots to our kids.

But did we?

Recently, our oldest daughter graduated from high school. To commemorate her accomplishment, Patti and I wrote her long letters from Mom and Dad. In those letters we walked down memory lane reflecting on and getting nostalgic about her eighteen years of life. As we reminisced, it dawned on both of us that while we gave the girl opportunities, we never gave the girl roots—at least not with respect to *place*. To date, she has lived in seven different homes and attended eight different schools in five different cities.

Contemplating the quasi-nomadic upbringing that we imposed on our daughter, Patti wrote in her letter from Mom, "I am so so so sorry . . . and you're welcome."

The "I'm sorry" part makes good sense. Moving of any kind is disorienting, especially in childhood. It uproots a child from friends, teachers, neighborhoods, and familiar spaces. It digs a hole in the heart, uprooting and rerooting like that. For better or for worse, our daughter's story has become the same as mine. It's a story with no lifelong friends or neighbors or houses from childhood. Instead, it's the story of a traveler.

What good could come from seven homes and eight schools and five cities in eighteen years? Why on earth would my wife feel compelled to say "You're welcome" right after saying "I am so so so sorry" to our daughter? I believe it's because regret and hope don't have to be mutually exclusive. In our daughter's case the two can run together for three reasons I can think of.

First, home is more than a place. Home is also the people you travel with and live alongside as you move from place to place. And, for those who travel with Jesus, family is everywhere— surrogate daughters, sons, brothers, sisters, mothers, fathers, grandmas, and grandpas await us in every city and town to which the church has been scattered.

Even more than this, *home* is three Persons versus a single place. The God of nomadic travelers *is* our home. He is the God of

Abraham, who left country and kindred and his father's house to the land that God would show him. He is the God of Israel, who wandered in the wilderness for forty years. He is the God of the Jews, who were taken captive to Egypt, Assyria, and Babylon after their homes were taken from them by conquest. And he is the God of Jesus Christ, who, in his most "displaced" moments, cried out to his Father for wisdom, comfort, and presence. This Father—this traveling God who also never leaves, and whose dominion and presence covers every single person, place, and thing—is also *our* Father. He is never away from us, and we are never away from him. Wherever we go, his goodness and mercy follow us for all of our days. If we ascend to heaven, he is there. If we make our beds in Sheol, he is there also. And? He is not merely with us; he is *within* us. He will never leave us or forsake us. In that sense, we are never *not* at home.

Second, while there are immense benefits to putting down roots in a particular place among a particular people (contrary to, and perhaps because of my immensely poor example, I highly recommend it), there are also some potential liabilities—namely, the narrowing, blinding effect of never being exposed to cultures, peoples, places, skin colors, economic brackets, dialects, philosophies, experiences, and perspectives that those who are *other* can offer us. For it is only in drawing near to *the other* that we gain a fuller appreciation of the *imago Dei*. For the *imago Dei* (image of God) is not contained in any single people group or place, but rather in the faces and stories and triumphs and sorrows of *every* nation, tribe, tongue, and generation. Rather than lock us down into a single place and perspective, the nomadic way increases our exposure and broadens our horizons.

Third, and perhaps most relevant, Patti's "You're welcome" to our daughter for the quasi-nomadic life that we have "given" her is that a quasi-nomadic life confirms that none of us is home—at least not yet. Said another way, traveling from place to place stirs our longing for the home that is truly *home*.

Indeed, none of us has arrived. Even the most rooted among us are, as the apostle reminds us, aliens and strangers who are traveling through a land that is, by its fallen nature, foreign to us. We are, as it were, *exiles*. The place that Jesus has gone and prepared for us is not here but *there*. Not even the faith heroes of Hebrews 11 got to see or experience the "better country" while they were living. So then neither should we expect to see or experience home fully or finally until Jesus returns. This is the same Jesus who will *make all things new* as he transforms this weary world into a garden city—new Jerusalem, with a tree rooted down deep, right in its center, planted there for the healing of the nations—that we will forever call *home*.

Until then, even the most solid homes and the deepest roots will merely be appetizers to prepare us for an everlasting feast, road signs to prepare us for an everlasting destination, temporary dwellings to prepare us for an everlasting home.

Like every good gift from God, the places and people that we call home are pointers, but they are not the point. Until we understand this, I daresay we will not only be wanderers but aimless and rootless ones. "Aim at heaven," C. S. Lewis said, "and you'll get earth thrown in. Aim at earth and you'll get neither."

Lewis also said, "If we find ourselves with a desire that nothing in this world can satisfy, the most probable explanation is that we were made for another world."

Lewis's observation, coupled with my own sometimes lonesome and sometimes wonderful nomadic years, makes me so grateful for writers like Jen Michel.

The book you hold in your hands is Jen's second book. I would be remiss not to also recommend to you, with highest praise, her first—*Christianity Today*'s Book of the Year, no less—

called *Teach Us to Want*. But this, Jen's second book, is like a buffet of appetizers, each of which points to the feast that awaits us at the banquet table of God. It is like a series of road signs, each one serving as a reminder that though we are still traveling, our final destination is just around the bend. It is like a series of stops along the journey—none of which we own but are merely paying rent, and yet all of which we are meant to savor—as each season and step gets us closer and closer to the home where Jews and Gentiles, Pharisees and prostitutes, smug sons and prodigals, urban dwellers and farmers, the rooted and the rootless will all find welcome.

Keeping Place is both memoir and rich biblical theology, and is, in all of its parts, an aroma of the home we've been made and are destined for. With wit, candor, a good bit of humor, and transparent glimpses into *her* home, her history, her travels, her travails, her worship, her marriage, her table, her rest, and her longings— Jen offers an oasis for all of us who are homesick. Most of all, she teaches us to better discern the sights, smells, and tastes of *home* that are all around us right here and right now. In other words, she helps us aim at heaven, so that along the way, a little bit of earth gets thrown in too.

I pray for you, and I pray for myself, that we would be given eyes to see as Jen does.

PREFACE

151 GLENDON AVENUE
TORONTO, ONTARIO

IT ALMOST FEELS LIKE DECEMBER in New Zealand," Caleb exclaims, taking off his shoes at our front door. Having recently moved to Toronto for a neurosurgery fellowship, he visibly mourns that his family's first Canadian Christmas, celebrated together with our family and other members of our church, is not the white idyll of greeting cards. Several months earlier, he, his wife, and his three children crossed continents and oceans, expecting to return home to a prestigious position at a renowned hospital. But the future ominously shape-shifts, dims, blurs. Professional doors close in New Zealand, and opportunity dries up. "We'll consider Australia next," Caleb explains. "Then Singapore."

Judith arrives next, bearing her promised plate of delicately decorated Christmas cookies in the shapes of angels and camels, bells and trees. Nearing seventy, Judith was widowed in middle age and left to raise her three boys without a father. She eventually remarried, though she and her second husband have recently separated for reasons she leaves silent. Alone, she bears the weight of a present that is neither divorce nor marriage. Her future pitches with uncertainty, even if her faith acts as admirably as sea legs.

Hannah and Solomon follow behind Judith. Born in Ghana, the couple grew up in London, living there until they moved to Canada, one week after their wedding. Six months after their international move, Solomon was diagnosed with stage 4 cancer; two years later, he lives a merciful and miraculous stay of execution. If Christmas marks a holy birth, it also signals, for this couple, God's gift of ongoing life. I ask the young, childless couple about their plans for the future, whether they'll stay in Toronto or return to London. Hannah hesitates before answering. "We're at home here. At least for now."

Andrea is last to arrive. The only Canadian to join our cosmopolitan group for Christmas dinner, like Judith, she comes alone. Her parents died months before her high school graduation; weeks later, her older sister, executor of the estate, ordered her out of the family home, refusing to pay her university fees. At eighteen, Andrea was marched forcibly into independence and solitary self-sufficiency; at forty, she's returned to Canada from Asia, where she spent the last ten years, her future buoying on the hope of reconciling with her siblings. "I'm giving it a chance," she says softly. *Home*, that is.

Around our dinner table at Christmas, these are the stories that home tells. Each inhabits a fragile in-between. Even our family, host of the occasion, lives a rented, expatriate life in

Toronto, the city where we chose to make our home after my husband was offered a corporate transfer. Like that of our guests, our future shimmers like a mirage. If we extend our arms, reaching for clarity, we grasp at the wind.

HOW DID WE GET HERE?

It wasn't difficult to move five years ago. My husband, Ryan, and I were raised in churches that valorized missionary service as the zenith of Christian devotion. In our mythologies of faith, uprooted trees were the most virtuous kind. We grew up in the incandescence of names such as Lottie Moon, Amy Carmichael, and Hudson Taylor. As children at Vacation Bible School we pooled our pennies to send the good news to the jungles of Ecuador, Papua New Guinea, and the heart of Africa. At missions conferences and revival services, the plaintive notes of "Just as I Am" wooed from the front, begging us to surrender all to Jesus. After all, even God's Son had no place to lay his head.

At twenty-two, a year after having served a summer together in Mali, Africa, with a team from Wheaton College, Ryan and I married under the banner of Psalm 67:

> May God be gracious to us and bless us
>   and make his face shine upon us, *Selah*
> that your way may be known on earth,
>   your saving power among all nations. (Ps 67:1-2)

We committed ourselves, as newlyweds, if not to vocational ministry, at the very least, to the ends of the earth. We believed that the nations bid us leave, not stay, and after several geographic moves, the nations eventually embraced us in Toronto. The winds of God's diaspora have blown us here.

In truth, I want the nations to impose a divinely linear line on our serial displacement. But I can't help also feeling like we are failing terrifically at stability, especially at the time when our oldest daughter, entering high school, is supposed to be needing it most. Every year, we depend on the Canadian powers that be to renew our visa and extend our stay, which is, of course, nothing like staying and everything like visiting. In my moments of in-between, I let myself wonder what it might have been like to cherish something other than change. What if we had stayed put? This book grows out of that anxious curiosity, if also the inevitable homesickness, which Frederick Buechner describes as the innermost heart of human desiring.[1] To be human, whether having moved or stayed, is to long for home.

Many of us seem to be recovering the sacred, if ordinary, beauty of place. Perhaps we're reading along with Wendell Berry, falling in love with Berry's small-town barber and Jayber Crow's small-town life. As Troy Chatham fells the final grove of trees on the family farm, destroying hundreds of years of memory in unrestrained greed, we discover the grief in losing connection to the land.[2] Or maybe we're simply reading our Bibles better, discovering that while we might wish to flatten Scripture to serve our didactic purposes, it rises up in flesh and sinew, muscle and bone: God's holy story is written in the lives of people and their places. Whatever the reasons, I hope that *Keeping Place* will have a part in the place conversation, offering hope to the wanderer, help to the stranded.

THE SHAPE OF THIS BOOK

To explore the meaning of home in part one, I share stories from my own life; offer up cultural, literary, and historical artifacts; and most importantly explore the storied landscape of the Bible, which insists on the gift of place and the welcoming love of a homemaking, housekeeping God. Home was one of humanity's first gifts. I've become convinced that what happens from Genesis to Revelation can be told as a *home* story: God makes a home, sinners take leave, and the Father bids our return. More than that, I believe that we must learn to share the gospel in this way. As civil rights activist John Perkins has written, "The job of an evangelist is to connect God's good news with people's deep yearnings."[3] From the Syrian refugee to the suburbanite, people are longing for a place to throw open the door and breathe in belonging. They are looking for home. While the average agnostic today is not necessarily looking for unimpeachable arguments for the existence of God, in their most private moments, they might admit to the transcendental longing expressed by agnostic author-philosopher Julian Barnes in his book *Nothing to Be Frightened Of:* "I don't believe in God, but I miss Him."[4]

Keeping Place isn't, however, only about the longing for home; it's also about its shared labor. There is work to be done in the world God has made and will remake; there is *housekeeping*, if you will. And this is the focus of part two of this book: how God's welcome inspires our work. It might be helpful to think of this book tracing the arc of a Sunday morning liturgy. If it opens with a call to worship the Homemaker, it ends with a commission to make a home for others in the world. In some sense every vocation is an act of homemaking and housekeeping because we are made in the image of a homemaking God.

Though her legacy was not explicitly Christian, Jane Addams, a social reformer in the late nineteenth and early twentieth century, took up housekeeping as I mean to primarily use it in this book. She founded the Hull House in Chicago in 1889, sensing that the industrialized American city had failed in the measure that it lacked "domesticity." Addams fought for immigrant rights, labor reform, juvenile justice, public housing and healthcare, and the Hull House became a cultural center and a safe haven for immigrants. In 1893, Hull House established a communal playground, reclaiming from unsanitary tenement buildings a safe place for recreation.

As the mission of Hull House expanded, so did its real estate. Addams hired the socially conscious architects Allen and Irving Pond to design the enlarged complex. Built like a university quadrangle with a courtyard at the center, the complex eventually included thirteen buildings, one of which was specifically designated for children. There, a nursery and kindergarten program provided education to disadvantaged children, and the Infant Welfare Society, a well-baby clinic, and a city dental clinic offered medical services and training for young mothers. Of Addams, the feminist scholar Glenna Matthews writes, "One could argue that the settlement-house movement itself, with its creative reform legacy, was a working-out of domestic feminist visions because settlement women sought to carry the values of home to slum-dwellers."[5] Addams became the first unofficial garbage inspector in Chicago, trailing the garbage inspectors "through alleys knee-deep in rotting food, beer, animal carcasses, and human and animal waste. Addams ensured that the city wards didn't avoid their duties in a neighborhood that was often ignored."[6] Though she was neither a wife nor mother, Jane Addams was a homemaker for Chicago's immigrant poor. She took up the embodied work of welcome; she labored for love. Similarly, Christian men and women, praying for God's kingdom to come on earth as it is in heaven, work to make it possible for all human beings to flourish—now and into eternity. Housekeeping, as an important dimension of the home story, insists that an in-between life must never be an idle one. To be blessed is to be sent.

No greater example can be offered than God's own incarnate Son, Jesus—who exchanged the glories of a heavenly home for the indignities of an earthly one. He healed the lame, forgave the sinner, cleansed the temple, and eventually surrendered himself to the public humiliation of Roman crucifixion because the world refused him welcome. In every act of what we might call the cosmic housekeeping, the divine body was implicated; salvation was no virtual affair.

On the night he was betrayed, Jesus took up a basin and a towel and washed the dirty feet of his disciples because he knew his home story: "that he had come from God and was going back to God" (Jn 13:3). As Jesus anticipated the cross, home was not only his confidence, it was also his commitment. We are servants in his stead.

This is not a book about women and women's work, although women do feature prominently in the stories the Bible tells about home. It is not primarily a book about marriage and family, although I am a wife and mother. Instead, this is book about witness and work: the witness of our God's welcome, the witness of our homesickness, and the ongoing witness and work of the church. As James K. A. Smith describes, we are "'narrative animals': we define who we are, and what we ought to do, on the basis of what story we see ourselves in."[7] Home is that story.

And we are its witness.

Part I

THE WELCOME
OF HOME

NOSTALGIA

The Longing for Home

**156 CHARJEAN DRIVE
JACKSON, TENNESSEE**

As a child in elementary school, I didn't play house. I kept it. Several times a week, I marched imperiously through the rooms with a laundry basket on my hip, rescuing stray books and orphaned socks. When the basket brimmed, I dumped the loot at the threshold of either my brother's or my parents' bedroom, a signal that careless housekeeping would not be tolerated. Never did I condescend to put anything away.

Such was my precocious, self-interested pleasure in wringing order out of chaos, a word that exaggerates the state of domestic affairs in my house growing up. My mother, a nurse, was hardly the worst of housekeepers. To her credit she maintained sanitary standards. But if things in our home were clean, they were not always neat. Furniture served alternate purposes for which they were not primarily intended. The microwave stored cookbooks. We left clean laundry for weeklong stretches on the Ping-Pong table and the couch. If there has been one method of house-keeping my mother consistently relied on, it is accumulation. Even as my mother and stepfather began downsizing in their retirement in the past year, the task of deciding what would stay and what would go proved Herculean. "What will I do about my Christmas dishes?" my mother asked me over the phone, grief ringing in her voice. The painstaking negotiation was not unlike a divorce settlement.

Once upon a time, in my cluttered childhood home, a laundry basket made the material world comprehensible. There was a place for everything, and everything in its place. Today, at home with my husband, five children, and our gray chinchilla, Gandalf, my domestic ambitions fail despite that I've labeled pantry shelves and paid generous sums for the performance of regular chores. Beds are haphazardly made. Someone absconds with the Scotch Tape. The glue disappears from the homework supply box, causing someone to shed crocodile tears over his inability to catalog the animals, which do and do not lay eggs.

The housekeeping suffers at my house. It suffers enough that my eleven-year-old daughter, a blond version of my younger self, scolds her twin brothers when they kick off their shoes in the mudroom, and shoes fly in opposite directions. "Didn't I just clean up?" she demands. Camille has a preternatural instinct for housekeeping.

Which may be another way of saying: she longs for home.

HUMANITY'S OLDEST ACHE

In an interview with the *New York Times,* Tiffany Watt Smith, author of *The Book of Human Emotions,* described her research on the role that language plays in our emotional lives. As Smith argues, words not only describe how we feel; they distinctly shape how we understand our feelings. In other words, a diminished vocabulary limits not just emotional self-expression but emotional self-perception. As complex emotional beings, we need nomenclature for fear and self-doubt, longing and desire. In short, we must be taught to explain ourselves to ourselves as well as to others.

"One of the emotions I became really interested in when researching the book was homesickness," Smith described in the interview. In the mid to late eighteenth century, homesickness was counted a credible source of physical ailment and even considered a possible cause of death. According to medical records, homesick patients experienced the expected symptoms of depression and fatigue, but they also suffered surprising physical ones, such as sores, pustules, and fevers. In severe cases, sufferers refused to eat, growing so weak as to eventually die. Their doctors labeled their deaths severe cases of *nostalgia*—from *nostos*, "homecoming," and *algia*, "pain." (The last mention of "nostalgia" on a death certificate was in 1918.)[1]

Nostalgia may have disappeared from our medical dictionaries, but we have not cured the ache for home. To be human is to know the grief of some paradise lost. Each of us—however happily settled—suffers a foreboding sense of rupture, as if we have been cut off from some hidden source of happiness. We are not unlike Lot, the nephew of Abraham, who parts from his uncle upon arriving in Canaan. When given first pick of the land, without any living memory of Eden, Lot scans the horizon and settles in the well-watered Jordan Valley because it bears resemblance to "the garden of the LORD" (Gen 13:10). Lot suffered nostalgia—or, as the French would say, *maladie du pays*: sickness of [a lost] country.

Biblical words related to *home* can denote physical dwelling, family household, material possessions, as well as geographical and social connections, but these words only hint at the emotional dimensions of the English word *home* and its cousins in German, Danish, Swedish, Icelandic, and Dutch. In these languages home connotes much more than geography and material reality; home also describes an emotional state of being. For the linguistic ancestors of the Old Norse, home, *heima*, means more than bricks and mortar. In part, its walls are safety, its windows, welcome. Provided there is intimacy and a sense of belonging, a home can be made in almost any place.[2]

Home represents humanity's most visceral ache—and our oldest desire.

THE WITNESS OF LITERATURE

Instinctive to the witness of Western Literature is the longing for home. Odysseus spent ten years fighting at Troy and another ten years getting home. His son, Telemachus, awaiting his father, defends his mother from the string of suitors wishing against Odysseus's safe return. He laments his father's exile. "How I wish I could have been rather son to some fortunate man, whom old age overtook among his possessions."[3] Telemachus senses the privilege of belonging to a place that serves as witness to our birth and spectator to our death, and understands that home is the place for being recognized, received, remembered. *Missed.* In the face of death, home, as perceived stability, is one hedge against the terror of the *réveil mortel*—the wake-up call to mortality. As writer Julian Barnes has put it in *Nothing to Be Frightened Of*, we live with "the vicious awareness that this is a rented world."[4] The grass withers, and the flowers fade: ours is an impermanent life. At the very least, home is a steadying consolation when the lights go out.

The novel is a powerful literary witness to human nostalgia: as philosopher and literary critic Georg Lukács has written, the novel is the great form of "transcendental homelessness."[5] This is to say that from *Don Quixote* to Don Delillo, the world's greatest writers are giving voice to our inexorable grief at *lostness* and our irrepressible joy at being found. Homelessness, whether physical or spiritual, is the terror of the elements and the threat of an angry sky. Home is the dry place we are all searching for. Humans need home.

Marilynne Robinson's third novel in the Gilead series, *Lila*, reprises the story of the Reverend John Ames from the perspective of his unlikely wife, who had been rescued as a feverish young toddler by a girl named Doll. "There were arms around her to let her know she was safe, and there was a whisper at her ear to let her know that she should not be lonely. The whisper said, 'I got to find a place to put you down. I got to find a dry place.'"[6] Doll makes a home for Lila on the run, and the only stability the two enjoy as drifters is their loyalty to one another.

Many years later, after Doll's death, Lila finds a ramshackle cabin at the edge of Gilead, where she makes a temporary home. Upon going into town to look for work, she makes John Ames's acquaintance. Seeing him thereafter only occasionally and taking strange initiative to tend the roses of his first wife's grave, Lila eventually tells Ames he ought to marry her. To the shock of the town, even his own, he does, and soon she conceives his child.

But neither John Ames nor Lila is convinced that she will stay in Gilead permanently, not when she has mastered the rituals of vagrancy and the reflexes of distrust. She has never had a home. Yet the old man is good to her. "The old coat he had put over her shoulders when they were walking in the evening was as good to remember as the time Doll took her up in her arms. She thought it was nothing she had known to hope for and something she had wanted too much all the same."[7] If Lila never held out real hope for having a home—that dry place out of the rain—it was also true there was nothing she had wanted more.

THE VOICE OF THE REFUGEE

Fiction isn't our only witness of home; the front page is. In the most recent European migrant crisis, for example, desperate families, forced by war and poverty, leave home. The tragedy of these asylum seekers isn't only material loss, although it certainly is not less than that. When they crowd into rafts and trains, when they walk for days, history heavy on their backs, even when they arrive by plane like the many Syrian refugees now arriving in Canada, they take the future into their hands, hoping to find safety and stability for their children. Sometimes their arrival is cheered by smiling crowds readied for the work of hospitality. Sometimes their assets are legally seized by the government as the price of their welcome.[8]

Seven months pregnant, Carolina, a young Palestinian woman, traveled to Toronto with her youngest daughter, leaving behind her husband and young son because there is "no work in Gaza. There is no life." Three years earlier Carolina had come to Canada as a married mother not yet twenty, intending to study English. One month after her arrival, she learned that she was pregnant, and after a semester of study, was forced to give up her academic scholarship and return to Gaza—though not before she gave birth to her daughter and secured for her a passport to a better life.

We met Carolina when she returned a second time to Canada last year on her not-yet-expired student visa. She and her young daughter arrived at the airport after days of bureaucratic hassle at the Egyptian border and an exhausting flight, towing a small suitcase and the dim hope that despite having no family member or friend to contact, someone would take them in. A police officer eventually directed them to a Christian refugee welcome center, and the young mother and child made a home there for their first several months on Canadian soil. When it came time for Carolina to give birth, the center directed her to the ministry of Safe Families Canada to help her find care for her daughter during her brief hospital stay. It was through this connection that our family began forging a friendship with Carolina and her two daughters—a friendship that is bearing witness to humanity's oldest ache. From Gaza to Gilead, we long for home.

The months unfurl, and Carolina awaits the decision of immigration officials. Carolina's daughters and son grow tall, and Skype provides a semblance of connection between husband and wife. But if Canada does not allow her to bring her husband and young son to Toronto, Carolina and her two daughters will return to Gaza and the hopelessness of unemployment, scarce electricity, and everyday violence. They will go home—if it can be called that. For as Kenyan-born Somali poet Warsan Shire describes:

> no one leaves home unless
> home is the mouth of a shark
> you only run for the border
> when you see the whole city running as well.[9]

WHERE'S HOME FOR YOU?

To the practical stranger who asks in the perfunctory overtures of acquaintance, perhaps noting the nasal quality of my vowels, I trace the rough contours of growing up in the States. My family crisscrossed the Midwest and South for my father's education and career advancement. Every three years we packed and unpacked life, chasing, like many American families, the tail of opportunity. Born in Indiana, I learned to love the ruddy soil and dogwood springs of Tennessee. But I never laid any real claim to place. As a child I had nine different addresses; as an adult I've had seven. Despite having married a man who was born and raised in the same Chicago suburb, I have shared my childhood transience with him and our five children like a pox. Five years ago we left our settled suburban life in the Midwest and became expatriates to Canada. Now home is nowhere. Or home is here. According to one's perspective.

At the very least, home would seem to be the logical place for burying my body, and some days I let myself wonder where I will be laid to rest. After their deaths when I was younger, my father and brother were interred in Columbus, Ohio, off Highway 23. When my father died and before my mother re-married thirteen months later, she reserved a contiguous plot for herself, leaving blank her half of their common headstone. Several weeks ago she texted pictures from the cemetery, which she had visited with my brother's son, who is himself a man now. They laid flowers at the graves: white lilies for my father, dead at forty-nine, and a multicolored bouquet for David, dead at twenty-three. I suppose room could be made for me in their company should Ryan outlive me, although he would have to impose upon my closest friend of more than twenty years, still living in Columbus, to tend the plot annually. But that's just it: without a home, everything is a possible imposition. One burden of homelessness is this: you're always a stranger, counting on someone's good graces.

THE OLD, OLD STORY OF HOME

Foxes have holes. Birds have nests. And as Scripture records, in the beginning, the sons and daughters of God had a warm, dry place to lay their heads. The God-before-the-beginning formed, from dust and bone, the first human family, to whom he played host and set a table for feasting. Genesis 1–2 records the acts of

God's prodigious hospitality when he satisfied the desires of his people, both with the gift of place and of his presence. Humanity's first home was a shelter from the rain. It was a home for sitting and staying a while. Nothing good was withheld from Eve and Adam in the *very* goodness of their first home, and at week's end, when the holy work of homemaking was finished, God "blessed the seventh day and made it holy, because on it God rested from all his work that he had done in creation" (Gen 2:3). Rest was the coda of the symphony. Men and women kept company with God, with the land, and with each other, and obeyed the unforced rhythms of work and worship, labor and leisure, ordained by God himself.

The biblical narrative begins and ends at home. From the Garden of Eden to the New Jerusalem we are hardwired for place and for permanence, for rest and refuge, for presence and protection. We long for home because welcome was our first gift of grace and it will be our last. The settings of our first home and our last home testify to the nature of the embodied story God is writing in human history. Because God's story begins in a garden and ends in a city, place isn't incidental to Christian hope, just as bodies aren't incidental to salvation. God will resurrect our bodies, and he will—finally—bring us home. As Craig Bartholomew, author of *Where Mortals Dwell*, concludes, "One of the glories of being human and creaturely is to be implaced."[10] The "fortune" of home, as Homer puts it, is the witness of Genesis and of Revelation. God will never leave any of his children to homelessness.

HUMANITY'S EARLIEST GRIEF

Home, in this first human story, is happiness. Strikingly, however, home isn't the setting of most of the biblical action. God's seventh-day rest in Genesis 2:1-3 is quickly appended by domestic rebellion when Adam and Eve break the one inviolable house rule: they eat from the tree of the knowledge of good and evil, and suffer banishment from the Garden. God sends the self-determined refugees eastward and posts an angelic sentry at the tree of life, rescinding their right of return. The very good home, which God has made for his people, stands vacant, its doors and windows shuttered.

If the Bible testifies to the joy of home, the bulk of the narrative witnesses to the grief of its loss. "Displacement is at the heart of God's judgment," writes Bartholomew, who suggests that the biblical drama can be divided into three acts: implacement, displacement, and reimplacement. After Genesis 3, the history of Eve and Adam's children strings together like one long farewell. In Genesis 4, Cain kills his brother in a jealous rage and is cursed to wander. In Genesis 6–9, a flood of divine wrath destroys people and place. Noah and his family are rescued from judgment, and as they emerge from the ark, they are commanded to fill the earth and make it home. But this beginning ends no more hopefully than the first. In Genesis 11, people once again dare to be like God and begin construction on the Tower of Babel. Their profane act of self-implacement is thwarted, and God scatters them, the construction site becoming a vacant urban lot—another spectacle of blight and abandonment.

The book of Genesis, after chapter 3, is not a record of rootedness but a narrative of movement and migration. Faith, in the lives of the patriarchs, is nomadic in nature. As the book turns to the Abraham story in chapter 12, it narrates, with Tolkien determination, the "quest for landedness."[11] The father of faith heeds God's call to uproot his family and leave Haran, traveling according to the promise of land and children. Nevertheless, though God leads, Abraham doesn't achieve sudden stability. No sooner do he and his household arrive than famine strikes, forcing their migration to Egypt (Gen 12:10-20). Once back in Canaan, Abraham must then part from his nephew, Lot, when they realize that the land cannot support both men's flocks and herds (Gen 13:1-13). When Isaac, the son of promise, is finally born to the aged couple, the family still isn't home. The text insists on impermanence: "And Abraham sojourned many days in the land of the Philistines" (Gen 21:34). Moreover, if this geographic drifting weren't troubling enough, in a haunting echo of Genesis 12, God calls Abraham to bind Isaac and slay him.

Ellen Davis, in her book *Getting Involved with God*, makes much of the parallels between the leaving God asks Abraham to do in Genesis 12 and the leaving required in Genesis 22. "Do you hear it, the same phrase 'get you going' that created the first great rupture in Abraham's life? Even the same three-beat rhythm is repeated before the boy is named."[12] Get you going—from your country, from your kindred, from your father's house; get you going—with your son, your only son Isaac, whom you love. In the life of Abraham *get you going* acts both as promise and peril, both as reward and risk. There is no sense of settledness in Abraham's story, according to the promise as God has given it. In fact, Abraham never fully inherits the land according to its divinely appointed boundaries. Indeed, at the time of his death Abraham owns just the deed of one small piece of property: a cave in the field of Machpelah, which he purchases for four hundred shekels as a burial plot for Sarah. When he negotiates the land contract, he emphasizes his outsider status: "I am a sojourner and foreigner among you" (Gen 23:4).

Abraham died clinging tenaciously to divine promissory notes. To some it may have looked a little like dying empty-handed. He'd been promised a home, but he hadn't received it—and neither would his son Isaac or his grandson Jacob. As the writer of Hebrews explains, "These all died in faith, not having received the things promised, but having seen them and greeted them from afar, and having acknowledged that they were strangers and exiles on the earth" (Heb 11:13). The patriarchs were pilgrims; they "look[ed] forward to the city that has foundations, whose designer and builder is God" (Heb 11:10). And as if to emphasize the forward-looking hope of these ancient people of God, the book of Genesis ends *in medias res*: "They embalmed [Joseph], and he was put in a coffin in Egypt" (Gen 50:26). Jacob is dead, Joseph is dead, and Canaan is a dim memory: home, for God's people, is a distant hope.

GOD'S WANDERING PEOPLE

Abraham's story is not anomalous; he is the father of God's wandering, wayward people, who despite the eventual provision of a promised home after four hundred years of Egyptian slavery choose exile. Israel ignores the ceaseless warnings of coming judgment, which portend forfeiture of the land because of their repeated rebellion. "How long, O LORD?" the prophet Isaiah asked, tiring of his own fire-and-brimstone preaching. God answers,

> Until cities lay waste
>   without inhabitant,
> and houses without people,
>   and the land is a desolate waste. (Is 6:11)

Though God gave form to formlessness and order to chaos at the beginning of the world, he reverses these acts in judgment, and like our first human parents, Israel is cast from God's presence because of their sin. They lose home.

As the book of 2 Kings concludes, nothing is left for Israel, not even the temple, after the Babylonian conquest in 587 BC. Zedekiah, the final king of Judah, is cruelly treated by the marauding invaders: he witnesses his sons' murders, and then his eyes are gouged out before he is led away to Babylon. God's gloriously gilded house, built by Solomon, is burned to the ground. The land and the people lament the loss of their home and God's home, but there is no immediate answer, for the heavens are barred, and God turns his face away, his wrath smoldering like hot coals. "The LORD did not turn from the burning of his great wrath, by which his anger was kindled against Judah. . . . And the LORD said, 'I will remove [them] out of my sight'" (2 Kings 23:26-27). And though a remnant does return and a replacement temple is eventually rebuilt, it is such a diminished version of its former splendor that "many of the priests and Levites and heads of father's houses, old men who had seen the first house, wept with a loud voice when they saw the foundation of this house being laid" (Ezra 3:12). Home was not the glory it once was.

Yet exile was no surprise chapter in the story of Israel. On the eve of crossing the Jordan River after forty years of wilderness wandering, God had predicted the calamity of Babylonian siege and Israel's dismissal from the land. Despite this and many centuries of prophetic warnings, God's people willingly forfeited the good gift of home. And yet, as measure of his characteristic steadfast love, as proof of his inclination toward relenting mercy, God reassured the people that homelessness would not be the end of Israel's story. Their fortunes would be restored (Deut 30:1-4). He would circumcise their hearts, and they would obey him rightly, making it possible for God to restore home to his people. Return, repentance, rest: these are the siren melodies of the prophets. For as long as there is a compassionate Father, there will be a home, a table, and a feast. This was Israel's great consolation: exile was the middle act of the drama, but it was not the final scene.

HAPPILY EVER AFTER

The nostalgic longing for home is an impulse of Eden. But not everyone is a believer in that primordial happiness. Some resist the idea that the world was ever enchanted. In his essay *The Myth of Sisyphus*, French existentialist Albert Camus admitted inhabiting a universe "divested of illusions and lights."[13] Like Nietzsche, he had dismissed the possibility of God and with him moral absolutes and transcendent purpose. Without God, there was not a place for everything, nor could everything have its proper place. In Camus's story, "a man feels an alien, a stranger. His exile is without remedy since he is deprived of the memory of a lost home or the hope of a promised land. This divorce between man and his life, the actor and his setting, is properly the feeling of absurdity."[14] The only dignity afforded to the actors in the play of the absurd was, according to Camus, their "freedom" to "live *solely* with what he knows, to accommodate himself to what is, and to bring in nothing that is not certain. . . . He wants to find out if it is possible to live *without appeal*."[15] In Camus's story, home is a fiction, and human beings must make courageous peace with eternal exile.

It is often supposed that despair is more intellectually credible than hope. According to the unbeliever, the Garden of Eden is just one more example of our great naiveté—the stuff of fairy tales. But in his memorable Andrew Lang lecture in Scotland on March 8, 1938, J. R. R. Tolkien defended the fairy tale against the accusation of primitivism. He was not persuaded, as was Andrew Lang, who had repopularized fairy tales in Victorian and Edwardian England, that the fairy tale belonged to prescientific eras. Rather, Tolkien believed that the fairy tale illuminated the nature of absolute reality. At its heart the fairy tale depended on the stubborn belief in the triumph of good over evil, something that Tolkien called "eucatastrophe" (*eu* for good, *catastrophe*, for overturning). Eucatastrophe, or the fairy tale's happy ending, was not to be confused with wishful thinking, for in Tolkien's words the happy ending is the "far-off gleam or echo of *evangelium* in the real world."[16] In other words, fairy tales tell not just good news but *true* news: death has no final word, evil is vanquished, justice reigns. This world of make-believe is, in fact, the world we all want. Moreover, according to the Christian, it is a real world we can call home.

The genre of fairy tale was, for both J. R. R. Tolkien and C. S. Lewis, both members of the unofficial literary society of the Oxford Inklings, naturally suited to their Christian belief that the sun would rise on a new world and that God's people would indeed live happily ever after. According to biographers Philip and Carol Zaleski, "The Inklings were, one and all, guilty of the heresy of the Happy Ending."[17] They rejected the modernist aesthetic of dissonance and estrangement, and instead longed to reclaim a world of beauty and goodness—a world of enchantment. In their stories of hobbits and orcs, fauns and beavers and Father Christmas, Tolkien and Lewis told the story of home as the Scriptures tell it: the world has fallen from its original perfection, but it will one day be restored. The enduring legacy of these stories testify to the resonance of their hope. Humans long for the thaw of winter and the return of the king. They want to go home.

Acquainted with the early grief of losing a mother, both Tolkien and Lewis knew the longing for a world in which death and injustice did not triumph. Devout Christians, both men knew the consolation of that desire in the story of Jesus Christ—because Christ has died, Christ is risen, Christ will come again. As the Zaleskis write, "When Sam Gamgee cries out, 'O great glory and splendor! And all my wishes have come true!' we are not in the realm of escapism, but of the Gospel, in all its strangeness and beauty."[18]

THE GOSPEL'S NEW BEGINNING

In John 1 the apostle reprises the language of Genesis 1 to announce a new beginning for the people of God: "In the beginning was the Word, and the Word was with God, and the Word was God. He was in the beginning with God." Jesus of Nazareth appears in the midday gloom of Roman-occupied Israel, just when the people of God despair of ever being home. God-made-flesh pitches his tent in their neighborhood; he *tabernacles* among them (Jn 1:14). And as if to erase any doubt about the nature of his mission, in his inaugural sermon, Jesus opens the scroll of Isaiah and inserts himself at the center of postexilic hope. He tells the gathered worshipers, "Today this Scripture has been fulfilled in your hearing" (Lk 4:21). Jesus declares an end to exile. He signals the beginning of a long-awaited homecoming.

This itinerant rabbi-healer travels the Judean countryside proclaiming the good news of home. And though the King of the Jews is eventually betrayed into the hands of the religious leaders of his day and Roman executioners, his followers witness to his resurrection. They write accounts, which clearly make him central to Israel's story. "Destroy this temple, and in three days I will raise it up," Jesus had said early in his ministry (Jn 2:19). "He was speaking about the temple of his body," the Gospel writer John concluded in the afterward realization to which he, and hundreds of other disciples, came: this is the Son of God—the fullness of God dwells in him. When Jesus' body was raised from the ruins, it formed, according to the apostle Paul, the cornerstone of the Christian church, "the household of God" (1 Tim 3:15). The body of Jesus was slain as the body of Isaac had not been in Abraham's story and delivered up for purpose of restoring humanity to God, humanity to home. Then, ascending forty days after his resurrection, Jesus insisted on the permanence of his presence in the language of home: "I will not leave you as orphans. . . . If anyone loves me, he will keep my word, and my Father will love him, and we will come to him and make our home with him" (Jn 14:18, 23). According to Holy Scripture, Jesus Christ makes possible the end of human estrangement.

The story of the Bible witnesses to the happy ending called home. For despite the human experience of estrangement in this middle act of the drama, the good news of the Christian gospel begins and ends with homecoming. Our anxiety to belong, our desire to be received, our hope for intimate embrace: these are met in the homemaking God of Abraham, who speaks the yes of his promises in Jesus Christ.

He seeks and saves the wandering lost.

ANGEL IN THE HOUSE
A Brief History

151 GLENDON AVENUE
TORONTO, ONTARIO

D on't forget to buy ingredients for the thumb-print cookies," Audrey reminds me.

From inside the van, she closes the door, and it disappears down the driveway. Behind the windows, the children wave enthusiastically at the diminishing form of their mother, standing in her slippers in the garage.

"You're not going?" our twin boys asked. They had learned that their father would travel with them to Chicago for their week-long school vacation while I stayed in Toronto. Their eyes widened at the thought of me haunting the house alone.

This is, of course, the irony of writing a book on home: mine had to empty in order to begin. The thrum and throb of family life—the arterial pulsing of the calendar—had to cease just long enough to let silence pool like afternoon sun, so that I, the cat, could be bidden to enter it. That space (and me in it) seems less self-indulgent than it once did.

Domestic ambition wasn't set before me as a child. Although I grew up in churches that affirmed traditional roles for women and men, I didn't grow up in a traditional family with a bread-winner father and a stay-at-home mother. My mother chose one of the three professions she remembers as being available to her as a high school graduate in 1963. Rather than becoming a secretary or teacher, she became a nurse. Sometimes she worked night shifts. She always worked summers, and as we got older, we were often left in the lonely care of Luke and Laura of *General Hospital.*

My mother did not work to afford luxuries like vacations and new furniture. She worked to put my father through graduate school. She worked to buy groceries. And sometimes, despite hard work and layaway plans, the dollars still failed to stretch. Once, at the Piggly Wiggly, after my brother and I had dutifully pushed the cart while my mother tapped at her handheld calculator, the groceries were scanned, and the cashier chirped, "That will be $53.17." Peering into her wallet anxiously, my mother reddened and shooed us from the store. We abandoned the cart without paying.

Although as a child and teenager I had not angled for baby-sitting jobs or pined to become a mother, the discovery of my first pregnancy, at twenty-six, was greeted with happy surprise. I ran upstairs from the basement bathroom, waving a pregnancy test, looking frantically for Ryan, and screaming, "Look!" Without warning, that stick inspired foreclosure on a former life. It was July, and I had been using my summer vacation from teaching high school to finish my master's thesis. Against the advice of my adviser and a former Wheaton College professor, who encouraged me to continue my studies, I finished my thesis but abandoned ambitions for a doctorate. Eight months later I quit my job. To write it now, the story belies a deliberateness it did not have at the time. Because life can be this ad hoc for all of us. We fall into our lives much more often than we decide them. As one biographer put it, "To the extent that we impose some narrative form onto our lives, each of us in the ordinary process of living is a fitful novelist."[1]

In one sense, the logistical impracticalities of commuting forty-five minutes to work, beginning every school day at 7:50 a.m., and coordinating daycare helped decide my near future, professional and domestic. My husband was also inordinately busy with his own career, his evenings and weekends dedicated to studying for his actuarial exams. But if I'm honest, my decision to leave the world of professional work and care for my children at home was motivated by more than pragmatism: it was also partial protest against the frequently empty feeling of my house growing up.

As a child I had wanted more of my mother's emotional availability. As a teenager, I had wanted to be picked up on time after practice.

A BRIEF HISTORY OF WESTERN DOMESTICITY

When feminism began taking hold in Britain in the 1970s, poetry publishing, which hitherto had been a predominantly male industry, began seeing the effects. More women were writing poems. However, their poetry seemed to quickly become marginalized as a specialist subcategory, and many blamed this on their choice of subject matter: they were writing about the home. "It extended boundaries," concedes Ruth Padel in *52 Ways of Looking at a Poem*. "But it also made it easier for male critics and poets to ignore 'women's poetry' as irrelevant, something they didn't need to read."[2] In other words, when women wrote about home and domesticity, some men reached for the remote. Even today, though men aren't scandalized for their interests in cooking, interior decoration, and home organization, many men don't naturally see themselves against a domestic backdrop—or as readers of a book about home. If this is regrettable, it also has historical explanation. For more than three hundred years, home has been the primary domain of women.

To assume, however, that home has always been a uniquely feminine place is to ignore an important history of the home. As an example, in eleventh-century France, in the absence of inns, restaurants, and other public meeting places, the homes of middle-class merchants and tradesmen were places of industry and business as well as residence. There were no private bedrooms in these long, narrow, two-storied town dwellings (or for that matter, bathrooms). Not uncommonly, families ate and slept with their children and servants, and households could easily number up to twenty-five people. Rooms of the house were not designated for particular purposes: a room used for morning study easily transitioned at midday to become a dining room, a desk transformed into a table. When European medieval painting showed women at work, "They were rarely alone, and inevitably their work occurred amid the activities of men—people talking, eating, conducting business, or lounging about."[3] The medieval bourgeois home was not a private setting for women (and children): it was a distinctly public space.[4]

Only as families began separating home and work (as did many European builders, lawyers, notaries, and civil servants beginning in the seventeenth century) did the home become a feminine space. This change, according to Witold Rybczynski, author of *Home: A Short History of an Idea*, is best illuminated in the domestic Dutch paintings of the time: "The Dutch were the first to choose ordinary women as their subject. . . . The world of male work, and male social life had moved elsewhere. The house had become the place for another kind of work—specialized domestic work—women's work."[5] Home, as the primary domain of women and the private setting for the family (the substitution of school for apprenticeship having made it possible for more children to be at home), was born in seventeenth-century Holland.

HOME AND FAMILY IN COLONIAL AMERICA

Similar domestic changes eventually took place in England's American colonies. In Colonial America before industrialization, husbands and wives worked at home together with the children underfoot. When women entered marriage, they entered their husbands' work and became their economic partners. They learned "new skills in butchering, silversmith work, printing or upholstering—whatever special skills the husband's work required," writes Nancy Pearcey.[6] If their husbands died prematurely, many women had mastered the requisite skills for running the family business independently and often financially self-sustaining into widowhood. Home represented a shared place of industry and business.

In *The Measure of Success*, authors Carolyn McCulley and Nora Shank highlight the surprisingly pragmatic economic arrangements of two traditional marriages before the Industrial Revolution—one Continental and one American. In Germany, at the age of forty-one, Martin Luther married (at her insistence) a former nun, Kate von Bora, whose rescue from a convent he had arranged after receiving her written pleas for his help. Luther was an overspender, and his income was becoming less and less reliable. But Kate transformed Black Cloister, the monastery that had been given them as a wedding present, into a thriving hotel. In addition to caring for their eventual six children and the six children of her husband's sister, "Kate used all her talents to make the Luther home self-supporting. Soon the Black Cloister became known as *Lutherhaus*. Kate became gardener, fisher, brewer, fruit grower, cattle and horse breeder, cook, beekeeper, provisioner, nurse and vintner."[7] At Black Cloister the Luthers hosted visiting scholars and students, and "the table she spread became an important place where ideas were shared and disseminated."[8] Kate Luther was a "homemaker," though not in the traditional sense we might use that word today.

In Colonial America Sarah Edwards' business acumen "enabled her husband to spend thirteen hours a day in his study."[9] Jonathan Edwards, the intellectual, theological giant of America's Great Awakening, depended heavily on the savvy of his wife's household management. In addition to caring for the eleven children she bore Edwards, Sarah oversaw the management and investment of their "10 acres of pasture, 40 acres of meadow, and 10 additional acres on a hill, as well as the £300 towards his house and £100 towards his salary."[10] The Edwards's home, like Lutherhaus, became a destination for young men hoping to learn from the great preacher and theologian, and Sarah Edwards was entirely responsible for overseeing not just the farm and the food, but also the production of the household soap, candles, and bedding.

In Colonial America home was a shared responsibility: mothers shouldered the economic burdens of the household alongside their husbands, and fathers participated with their wives in childrearing responsibilities. As a study of sermons and literature during this time period bears out, fathers were never excused from the domestic sphere but held primarily responsible for it. Parenting advice, delivered from the pulpit, was addressed to fathers, something that would no longer hold true by the mid-nineteenth century. Seventeenth-century Puritan Cotton Mather described his approach to bringing up his children "in the discipline and instruction of the Lord" (Eph 6:4): "I first beget in them a high opinion of their father's love to him, and of his being best able to judge what shall be good for them."[11] Because industry was located in the home and its outbuildings and fields, fathers had opportunity for direct and daily influence over their children, and they were expected to exercise it as a form of Christian duty. Husbands and fathers understood the importance of their presence at home.

THE GOLDEN AGE OF DOMESTICITY

The roles of wives and husbands, mothers and fathers, began changing as America itself rapidly changed between 1780 and 1830. Industrialization shifted the economic locus of activity from the home and family farm to the factory (and eventually, the office). This change did not, however, immediately devalue the role of women and the importance of the home. For a period of time, which some historians such as Glenna Matthews, author of *Just a Housewife*, call the Golden Age of Domesticity, mothers gained in moral stature, and the home gained in political importance. As pioneers moved westward and factories rose on the American landscape, these changes were seen as portents of moral and social disintegration in America—and home, a measure of stability. What the home had ceded in economic function, it gained in transcendence; what the Republican mother lost in economic participation, she had gained in moral authority.

Harriet Beecher Stowe, author of the most historically significant and bestselling novel of the nineteenth century, *Uncle Tom's Cabin*, embodies these changes for American women. Her notable influence (Abraham Lincoln reportedly said upon meeting her, "So this is the little woman who made this big war") was not gained *despite* her domestic roles, though she herself complained about the onerousness of the housework and childrearing for which she and her husband could afford no help. While Beecher Stowe wished for more time to write, her role as housewife gave her the necessary political and social cachet to argue persuasively against the evils of slavery. "The political impact of *Uncle Tom's Cabin*, filled as it is with domestic imagery, demonstrated how the influence of home on the world could manifest itself."[12] In an age when the home was esteemed, Stowe's hearth was a source of political capital. Many other American housewives and mothers of the time similarly lent powerful, public voices to causes like the abolition of slavery, temperance, and women's suffrage.

HOME IN MODERN AMERICA

Unfortunately, the domestic bubble of the nineteenth century burst in the twentieth century as America came of age and the Republican spirit was crushed by big steel, big oil, and big finance.[13] Moreover, Charles Darwin, who claimed that women were biologically inferior to men and that their relative confinement to the home thwarted the evolutionary process of natural selection and kept them from improvement, vanquished the virtues of home.[14] Additionally, as the American home industrialized further, the role of the housewife became less productive: labor-saving devices like the electric iron, the sewing machine, the vacuum cleaner, and the electric washing machine saved enormous amounts of time.[15] The marketing to advertise these new products created a new culture of consumption, earning the housewife the title "Consumer in Chief."[16] The home was becoming less and less a place of production and more a place of consumption, and while new technologies spared women domestic effort, it also deskilled many tasks and drained creative satisfaction from their labor.[17]

The most consequential technological change for housewives in the twentieth century wasn't, however, the bevy of shiny new appliances. Rather, it was the emergence of the suburbs mid-century and the development of the highway system, two phenomena that contributed to the average housewife's social isolation. The middle class was fleeing the city, leaving behind richly communal lives, and transplanting itself into communities built predominantly not for the pedestrian but for the car. Women, cloistered in empty homes through long stretches of daylight, suffered from the lack of human contact, which they originally had enjoyed when home and work were organized more communally. Anne Sexton, 1950s housewife and Pulitzer prize–winning poet, betrays the bitterness of that newfound suburban alienation: "Until I was twenty-eight I had a kind of buried self who didn't know she could do anything but make white sauce and diaper babies. I didn't know I had any creative depths. I was a victim of the American Dream, the bourgeois, middle-class dream."[18] It was into this despair of Sexton's and other American housewives that Betty Friedan and her 1963 feminist classic, *The Feminine Mystique*, spoke.

Friedan seemed to have named the existential banality of many American housewives, giving women the freedom to say, "'I want something more than my husband and my children, and my home.'"[19] The letters of gratitude, which Friedan received, have been archived at Radcliffe's library in Boston, and they testify to the deluge of domestic relief for her book. But not all women, of course, embraced Friedan's conclusion that the American housewife needed liberation from her boredom. One example of bewilderment came from humorist Erma Bombeck, who had married in 1948 and left her career as newspaperwoman when she and her husband adopted their first child. In 1964, when her youngest was off to kindergarten, she reentered the work force, becoming a syndicated columnist within three weeks of her return.

When Bombeck and her friends attended a lecture given by Friedan in Columbus, Ohio, she described hearing Friedan tell the women they were living lives of quiet desperation. "'There was some truth to what she was saying,' recalled Bombeck, but on the whole Friedan was 'counting an anger among midwestern women that didn't yet exist. . . . I had a life going here. Maybe it needed work, but I had a husband and three kids whom I loved and I wasn't ready to discard anything.'"[20]

AN INHERITANCE OF AMBIVALENCE

This very cursory history of domesticity begins to frame the modern conversation about home. Many men have learned to assume that domestic responsibilities belong to their mothers and sisters and wives. A woman's place is the home, and they consider themselves woefully clumsy intruders.[21] Meanwhile, many modern women such as Caitlin Flanagan, frequent writer for the *Atlantic* and author of numerous books, inherit their domestic roles with a fair degree of ambivalence. We love—and loathe— "our inner housewife."[22] On the one hand, we are not the utterly unselfish "angel in the house," immortalized in Victorian England by Coventry Patmore's poem, who always chooses the leg of the chicken. On the other hand, we still value domestic sacrifice.[23]

As an example of modern women's contradicted desires, in her book *To Hell with All That*, Flanagan describes the maudlin eulogy she delivered at her mother's funeral: "All I could think about was what a wonderful thing it had been to be raised at home, by a mother who loved me."[24] Flanagan is notably grateful for her housewife mother, whose consecrated life work was making a home for her husband and children. Nevertheless, despite her heartfelt gratitude and admiration, Flanagan did not choose to follow in her mother's footsteps. In fact, she confesses to a good deal of suspicion about housekeeping, which she fears will prove to be a trap, "capable of snaring my ambition and worldly talent."[25] Flanagan wants the home that she had as a child, but like many of Friedan's children, she is less willing to make it herself.

The historical overview of home provides important context for the pressing task of biblical exegesis. If we come to the Bible looking to answer questions regarding home (and our place in it), we are best served by understanding our cultural assumptions, especially when approaching the only verse in Scripture that commands women to work at home (cf. Titus 2:5). In the passages most commonly used for defending strict gender roles in the family and church (e.g. Gen 1 and 2, Prov 31, Eph 5, Titus 2), none explicitly insist on the home as the "woman's place." As we've seen, this is a more recent development of the Industrial Revolution. Moreover, as Gail Collins argues in her book, *When Everything Changed*, the traditional arrangement of breadwinner husband and housewife has been a middle-class ideal. "In truth, the social rule that mothers should stay at home with their children had seldom been applied to poor women. After the Civil War, white Americans in both the North and South denounced black families in which only the husband worked. And from the time there were factories in American cities, there were women, many of them mothers, working in the assembly lines."[26] Without economic means, a woman has never enjoyed the luxury of deciding whether or not (or how little or much) she will work. To be "at home," as a woman, is an exercise of material privilege. And this begs us to let the Bible—and not our privilege—speak.

THE BIBLICAL COMMAND OF HOME

According to Scripture, home is shared human work. The most conservative reading of 1 Timothy 3, understood as a qualification for a male elder or pastor, confirms the necessity of active male participation in the domestic sphere. The man who presumes to manage the affairs of the church must capably manage the affairs of his own household (vv. 4-5). Moreover, leadership over God's people, which functions as God's household, does not require business savvy but moral probity and relational skill. An elder, or overseer, must be hospitable and gentle, traits most would traditionally consider as feminine qualities. He must not cede parenting responsibility to his wife but rather must be directly involved in the rearing of his children, "keeping his children submissive" (v. 4). Interestingly, it is his domestic abilities, in addition to his moral qualities, which are his qualifying grounds for ministry. "If someone does not know how to manage his own household, how will he care for God's church?" (v. 5). Should a man fail in his housekeeping, he will not be considered worthy of the position of elder.

The criteria for qualifying elders are not unlike the virtues of godly women in Titus 2, a passage frequently cited by some to defend the home as a woman's place. In his letter to Titus, Paul tells his young apprentice to instruct older women to "train the young women to love their husbands and children, to be self-controlled, pure, working at home, kind, and submissive to their own husbands, that the word of God may not be reviled" (vv. 4-5). With the exception of being "submissive to their own husbands" and "working at home" (the latter suggesting the forbiddance of idleness), this list sounds strikingly similar to the elder qualifications in 1 Timothy 3, both in substance as well as rank. As Kent Hughes writes in his commentary on the Pastoral Epistles, "The emphasis . . . is not on the location of a wife's work but on being productive in the normal occupations of a wife each day."[27] This passage, as well as 1 Timothy 3, does not insist that home is the unique charge of women. Rather, both suggest that domestic responsibilities are common to every human being and essential to a life of integrity.

God calls all his people to a holy integrity between their public and private lives. Home is a human calling because none of us is permitted the luxury of existential compartmentalization. Consider Christ's example as he hung from the cross. When effecting the public, cosmic act of human salvation, Jesus tended to private caregiving concerns. Jesus beheld Mary, his mother, standing in a cluster of loudly weeping women. His adoptive father, Joseph, was dead, and as the eldest son, charged with the responsibility of caring for his mother, he understood the threat his own death posed to her welfare. Struggling to breathe and bear up under the weight of human sin, Jesus entrusted the care of his mother to John (Jn 19:26-27). From the cross Jesus the Savior was also Jesus the Son. He demonstrated that each of us must shoulder the burden for "home." Our domestic responsibilities matter to God, for they testify to the seriousness of our faith. Paul put it as baldly as this in 1 Timothy 5:8: "But if anyone does not provide for his relatives, and especially for members of his household, he has denied the faith and is worse than an unbeliever." To ignore home is to deny God.

In addition, consider also one of the first decisive acts of the Christian church. When the Greek-speaking disciples began complaining that their widows were being overlooked in the daily distribution of food, the apostles appointed a group of men (not women) "full of the Spirit and of wisdom" to "*serve tables*" (Acts 6:1-6). The apostles did not intend to abandon their primary calling to preach the Word, but neither would they abide the breach of domestic duty. They knew that the family of God must receive the care that God their Father intended. In a very sacred sense, the male apostles were taking care of the housekeeping, affirming that the *table* is as central to Christian life as the *pulpit*.

God calls each of his children to a life that coheres in love. In the ambitious choreography of our days, we must fully consecrate every bead of sweat, wherever it falls—home or office, factory or school—to the glory of Christ and the good of our neighbor. Each of us, male and female, shares in the responsibility for home.

THE GOD WHO DOES WOMEN'S WORK

While home has not always been considered the domain of women, certain domestic tasks—gathering water, cooking, serving, and cleaning—have historically been (and in many parts of the world, still are) the responsibility of wives and mothers, daughters and sisters. Perhaps to our surprise, however, the God of the Bible does this women's work. *He keeps house.* And no doubt this is the strongest case for insisting that a book on *home* is a book for both women and men alike. If God does the work of women—and salvation can be compared, for example, to childbirth (Is 42:14) and the act of sweeping a floor (Lk 15:8-10), we are compelled to learn and speak the language of redemption as God himself speaks it. Should we fail to make use of the domestic imagery God offers to us in Holy Scripture, both for understanding who he is and the nature of his seeking-saving mission, we might wonder whom we cut off from the stories home tells.

In Isaiah 42 the God of judgment and mercy is not only likened to a "man of war" (v. 13), he is also compared to a woman in labor.

For a long time I have held my peace;
   I have kept still and restrained myself:
now I will cry out like a woman in labor;
   I will gasp and pant. (v. 14)

Written to the Jewish exiles in Babylon, the prophet Isaiah reminds God's people of their reliable hope: he is the "I Am God" of Abraham and Moses. Their story of estrangement from the Promised Land—and the Promiser—has not yet ended; God is declaring "new things" (v. 9). But Israel is not powerful enough to effect its own rescue. Instead, God must himself take up its cause. "The LORD goes out like a mighty man, like a man of war he stirs up his zeal" (v. 13). God declares that he will fight for his people's redemption and return. Nevertheless, God's zeal for Israel isn't only militaristic; it is also maternal. God brandishes a sword, but he also bears a child.

As Lauren Winner points out in *Wearing God*, the focus of Isaiah 42:14 is on the *sound* of God's labor. In this verse Isaiah uses three words that pertain to breath. According to Winner, the first—*pa'ah*—is best translated "groan" or "bellow."[28] The other two words indicate that God gasps (*nasham*) and pants (*sha'aph*).[29] Why, we might wonder, would the emphasis of this childbirth imagery be on its sound? Winner reminds readers that breathing is a technique women use to manage the pain of childbirth. "Mooing was the only sort of deep moaning noise that made my whole body feel good," one women tells her.[30] In other words, the sound of God's labor is the evidence of his pain. God bellows and gasps and pants to deliver his people unto salvation. The rescue of Israel is not bodiless or painless. God suffers like a woman squatting in childbirth. He writhes for the sake of redemption. This image of God laboring in childbirth points centuries forward to the bruised, battered, and bloody body of Jesus

Christ and the anguish of the cross. To ignore the laboring God of Isaiah, in other words, makes it easier for us to sanitize the gospel—and forget that the good news of home was bought with blood and bleats.

In the most famous of Jesus' parables there is also important domestic imagery. Sandwiched between the more familiar of the vignettes (the shepherd and the father) is the story of a woman, who is both scandalized and saved by her housekeeping. In an act of carelessness she loses a drachma, equivalent to a day's wage, in between the basalt stones of the floor. She trims the lamp, which floods the dim interior of her home with light, and sweeps carefully in the hopes of finding it. Her domestic method is, as Jesus describes, "diligent" (Lk 15:8). To her delight she finds the lost coin, and, in visible relief and gratitude, the woman calls together her friends and village neighbors to share the story of her good fortune (v. 9). Inconspicuously, salvation is secured at the bristles of a broom.

Jesus is teaching his listeners something surprising about the action of God: salvation is not unlike women's work. God is the finder of lost things, and that finding is owed to acts that look as menial as housekeeping. "It is as though God cannot be portrayed simply in terms of the shepherd, a man of daring and energy, but also must be thought of in terms of a woman who is upset by her loss, and who seeks the lost coin with the fastidious, meticulous care that the tradition, andocentric by habit, is apt to forgo," writes Kenneth Bailey in *The Good Shepherd*.[31] Jesus chooses to describe God's nature and God's mission in ways that both men and women will understand: he is a shepherd seeking lost sheep; he is a woman performing household chores. There is bold strength in the divine acts of salvation; there is also humble service.

As Bailey argues, Jesus' parable of Luke 15 follows the careful pattern of the nine biblical texts on the good shepherd beginning with Psalm 23, which includes references both to God's (masculine) shepherding and God's (feminine) hospitality. "The Lord is my shepherd," verse 1 assures. In this way he is our protector and defender, ready to brandish his rod and staff to warn off predators and thieves. But just as Isaiah was not content to limit himself to images of brute strength, David also includes a more feminine reference for the action of God. "You prepare a table before me in the presence of my enemies," David sings, ascribing to God the work of meal preparation (v. 5). "To 'prepare a table' means 'to prepare a meal,'" Bailey explains. "Middle Eastern people eat without using individual plates and eating utensils. . . . As regards the food, servants and women prepare it. The master of the house *provides* the food, he does not *prepare* it."[32] God, the defender, makes it possible to eat in the presence of enemies; God, the preparer of food, makes it possible to eat.

Little wonder that each of the three stories in Jesus' parable end in feast. A shepherd finds his lost sheep, and a woman finds her lost coin: both gather their friends and family to share in the good news. A father welcomes the return of his lost son, and he kills the fattened calf and throws a party fit for a king. These are some of the happy endings of salvation, and they all take place at home. We owe them our attention because they are the images Jesus himself takes up to call the lost: both those lost in the house (in this case, the Pharisees, who presumed mistakenly on God's favor) as well as those wandering in the far country (the tax collectors and sinners, who had misspent the inheritance). To help each of us understand our own lostness, we have to lean in to hear the story of home.

Home is a human place. Instinctively, each of us, male and female, knows the sound of its welcome—and the joy of our possible return.

3

TAKEN IN
The First Maker of Home

927 NORTH CHESTNUT
PALATINE, ILLINOIS

For weeks my husband, Ryan, and I entertain window salesmen, some of whom direct their pitches directly at Ryan, forgetting that I am a wage earner. We politely show them the door. But when a bespectacled, slightly balding man enters our house and thrusts his hand first in my direction, nodding, "Nice to meet you," I implicitly trust him before he has ever opened the thick, padded binders brought along for display. He recommends casement windows for the living room, double hung for the dining room, and awning windows for the master bedroom. We agree, and spring arrives. A crew of men removes the windows and their peeling sills, and for the first time, a breeze blows through our 1950s ranch.

Replacing the windows that had been painted shut by the former owners would be the most expensive home improvement project we ever undertook in our first home. And there wasn't any real guarantee we will be staying. "It's really only two bedrooms, you know?" my mother-in-law had tried to forewarn when we fell in love with 1,100 square feet on a gray day in February. But we weren't planning for babies. Guests of course, and for them we had adequate room in the finished basement. Ryan and I were in our mid-twenties, barreling through the beginnings of our careers. Family was a faint figure on the horizon—or rather, the state of affairs next door, where four-year-old Jonathan, whose steel-trap memory for the food preferences of dinosaurs, and his brother, lived.

For nearly three more years we didn't think of where we might put the children in our little house four blocks north of the library, even if I did indulge domestic zeal. I stripped wallpaper, painted the kitchen, borrowed a sewing machine from a neighbor to make blousy curtains for the dining room double hungs. I cooked regular meals for guests. We gathered my graduating high school students on the spacious deck as each school year ended, and lasted long evenings with friends under our brass chandelier and on our hand-me-down couches. From the day we moved in with the help of friends, who stopped to play an impromptu basketball tournament in the driveway after the truck was unloaded, the little gray house warbled its hello. Nine-twenty-seven Chestnut was home.

And finally, in March snow, we carried her home, two weeks past her due date: Audrey Grace, our first child. Within hours of our arrival we called the hospital hotline, reporting vague symptoms like "persistent crying" and "inability to fall asleep." For months I wore motherhood like a borrowed pair of (maternity) pants—ill-fitting and ugly. I suffered crying jags. I spent entire days in my pajamas. Two weeks into the ordeal, a neighborhood friend, mother of three, dropped off dinner before lunchtime and noticed my swollen eyes and my haphazardly buttoned shirt. She patted my back consolingly and assured, "It's this hard for everyone." The nights wore long. The prayers wore longer still as I sat on the floor of Audrey's nursery, rocking her cradle and fearing the indulgent act of picking her up.

Maybe the happenstance of having become parents has fortified affection for the little gray house on Chestnut for which we began planning an addition, even a second story. I only know it's the home I want to drive by slowly when more of life is behind than ahead. And if the children beg for a story, as long as patience sustains their interest, I'll let myself begin the history.

Of home.

HOME COMFORTS

After an affair and public divorce, Sandra Tsing Loh published an essay in *The Atlantic* titled "The Weaker Sex," claiming that the new household economics have made today's women "unwifeable."[1] Because the modern woman has achieved a new level of financial independence (in nearly 40 percent of marriages today, wives out-earn their husbands), Tsing Loh says they don't need men as they once did. In that vein the author raises a toast to her other DPM (divorced professional mother) friends, and they cheer what Hanna Rosin calls in her book "the end of men."[2] But there's a rueful sound in Tsing Loh's voice, especially when she describes the existential crisis of opening the refrigerator door.

> Day by day in our frenetic, chaotic modern homes, how many of us become inexplicably unglued, suddenly losing our equilibrium in a disproportionate vale of anguish, as

we open our refrigerator door . . . and confront the spillage from the leaking Ziploc bag or the microwave-deformed GladWare that forever will not close. On the one hand, these are a simple technical malfunction; on the other, they are another small but precise omen pointing to a world without the deep domestic comforts—and care, and arts— not of our mothers (many of whom were in a transitional leaving-home-to-go-work generation) but of our grand-mothers. No one is taking care of us! No one![3]

The "technical malfunction" of the GladWare and the absence of anyone to clean up the spill of the leaky Ziploc bag isn't tan-tamount to nuclear proliferation, but the encroaching chaos of sticky refrigerator shelves points to a palpable, ominous absence. Tsing Loh laments a world without housekeeping. No one is taking care of us!

Tsing Loh admits that her professionally work-weary world differs substantially from the domestic world of her grand-mothers, which she wistfully recalls in terms of "the homemade chicken soup with fresh-from-the-garden parsley, the warm strawberry crumble cake in the afternoon on a rolling glass tray, the doilies on couch arms, the polished chiming grandfather clock."[4] In her grandmothers' era, someone had been tasked with the spit and polish of life. Meals were made from scratch; they were served hot. Most importantly, all that good food presumably served up an invitation to the family to gather. And while there is certainly no sense in Tsing Loh's essay that she pines for the 1950s, the recognition of what's missing today—at home— unwittingly dampens her twenty-first-century self-congratulations.

In her book *Home Comforts*, Cheryl Mendelson attempts to rekindle the emotional, social value of housekeeping. Acknowl-edging the complicated relationship modern women have with domesticity, she opens her book with a confession: "I am a working woman with a secret life: I keep house."[5] Mendelson had been raised to become a rural farm wife and was schooled in the domestic arts by her grandmothers (who dueled considerably on best practice). But as she describes it, she eventually "made a youthful marriage to a man who ardently disliked domestic life."[6] Their lives were predictably careless in the care of home, and her husband's disinterest in housekeeping hadn't bothered her until the day Mendelson returned home to the sight of three dogs, wet and muddied, lying in their unmade bed. They divorced, and Mendelson returned to law school, where she unconventionally experienced a domestic reawakening.

"An off-and-on lawyer and professor in public, in private I launder and clean, cook from the hip, and devote serious time and energy to a domestic routine not so different from the one that defined my grandmothers as 'housewives,'" writes Mendelson, recognizing the eccentricity of her educated passion for home comfort.[7] Her book is an ambitious project for systematically teaching the care of a home. (Chapter 32 is devoted to the discussion of "aprons, rags and mops.") Nevertheless, Mendelson aims at more than how-tos. She wants to recapture more of the intimacy of housework—and less of the drudgery. She positions her book as exploring not just the proper methods of housekeeping but also the meaning.

The "intelligence" behind a well-kept house isn't fastidiousness, argues Mendelson, and hospitality cannot be measured in culinary skill. "If you cannot boil an egg or make a bed," writes Mendelson, "but you can and do make a nice cup of tea or coffee on the right occasion and serve it appealingly, you have gone farther toward making a good home than many a gourmet cook or compulsive housecleaner."[8] To be sure, a homemaker will find pleasure in wringing order from chaos and likely appreciate the principles of good architecture and interior decoration. But more than architecture and aesthetic are required for making a home; more than form and function are to be considered.

Most of all, a homemaker must love guests: "Empathy is the form of intelligence that creates the feeling of home."[9]

GOD AS HOMEMAKER

In Genesis 1–2, God makes a home for his people. From the primeval wilderness and wasteland God begets beauty and form, building the grand house called Earth. God's creative acts are not simply intended for the sake of aesthetic but as joyful preparation for God's children, who arrive at the threshold of the world on the sixth day. For while God deserved a universe befitting only himself, though he could have rightfully created galaxies whose only purpose was to showcase his glory, he created an oxygenated world—*because it suited us.*

The first, second, third, fourth, and fifth days in Genesis 1 are a literary crescendo recording the flurry of God's purposeful hospitality. God murmurs multiple times, "It is good," illustrating that he is pleased with his housework. On day one, the light and darkness are good (v. 4); on day three, the dry land, the seas, and the vegetation are good (vv. 10, 12); on day four, the sun, moon, and stars are good (v. 19); on day five, the taxonomy of animals is good (v. 21); on the sixth day, the creatures bearing the image of God, along with all that God has made, are very good (v. 31). However, on day two, when God separates the waters from the waters and creates the sky, he remains strangely mute (vv. 6-8). Only in this instance does God refrain from commending his work as good.

"The reason," writes John Sailhamer, in his commentary on Genesis, "is that on that day nothing was created or made that was, in fact, 'good' or 'beneficial' for humanity. . . . The land was still 'formless;' it was not yet a place where a human being could dwell."[10] According to Sailhamer, "good," as measure of God's approbation, was not a generic comment on the earth's form; it was a particular commendation of the habitability of the earth as a warm, dry place. In other words, creation was only good insofar as it could be *home* to humanity.

In Genesis 2 a second version of the creation narrative begins, and our beginnings are viewed from a different angle. In Genesis 1 humanity is set against the larger cosmological backdrop of "the heavens and the earth." In Genesis 2 the camera focuses more narrowly, and the first humans are "placed" somewhere particular—in a garden (v. 8). As Andy Crouch observes, Genesis 1 paints "creation in its totality," Genesis 2, the "immediate neighborhood."[11] Historically, scholars disagree if the Garden of Eden represents some untouched, untamed wilderness land or whether it approximates a cultivated garden typical of wealthy ancient Mesopotamian estates. If it's the latter, "what we have, then, rather than an image of primitivism, is one of an area that is bounded, probably by walls; carefully landscaped; and intensively cultivated with orchards and the like," writes Craig Bartholomew in his book *Where Mortals Dwell*.[12] But whether divine attention has been paid to hewing geometric pattern from the landscape or whether the garden grows beautifully wild, either way there is important textual emphasis on the word *put* in Genesis 2:8 and 15. This word speaks to God's intentional hospitality in his creative acts—and his world as "home."

The first time the word is used in verse 8 it signifies the most common use of *put*. Much like we put our shoes in the closet (or *should* put our shoes in the closet), God put Adam in a garden. In verse 15, however, the Hebrew word has more significant meaning. As Sailhamer notes, it is a word that can represent

God's "rest" or "safety." As examples of other uses, God "put" Lot outside the city before he rained sulfur and fire on Sodom (Gen 19:16); God "put" the Israelites in the Promised Land as a gift of "rest" (Deut 3:20; 12:10; 25:19).[13] Used in this way, the word signals the sheltering love of God and his paternal impulse to protect and provide for his children. God put Adam and Eve in the garden much like a mother swaddles her newborn baby and puts the child in the cradle. *You're safe*, she shushes.

This Hebrew word for *put* can signify not just safety and rest, but also dedication to God. As examples, the manna was "put" in the ark of the covenant (Ex 16:33-34); the high priest "put" on his linen garments when approaching the Most Holy Place (Lev 16:23); the chieftain staffs were "put" in the tent of meeting as a test of divinely invested authority (Num 17:4). Sailhamer argues that the author of Genesis intends both meanings in Genesis 2:15: "The man was 'put' into the Garden where he could 'rest' and be 'safe,' and the man was 'put' into the Garden 'in God's presence' where he could have fellowship with God."[14] Home is always more than physical shelter from the rain; it must also necessarily be a place for humanity to keep company with God. Home is for holiness.

God had a clear purpose for putting humanity in a garden beyond mere enjoyment of the scenery. As Genesis 2:15 indicates, "The LORD God took the man and *put* him in the garden of Eden to work it and keep it." God did not make a home for his children and leave them to idleness. Rather, he commissioned them with priestly work. Although translations have, from the second century BC, rendered "to work and to keep" as actions related to the care of the garden, some (like Sailhamer) argue that it is better translated, "to worship and obey."[15] As if in keeping with this translation, verses 16 and 17 outline the specific commandment God gives to Adam: he may eat of every tree of the garden but one. Humanity's first home was built on the principles of God's generosity—but this must not be confused with God's permissiveness. Home had one important rule, which God expected his children to heed. As the text makes clear, God did not forbid his children the fruit of the knowledge of good and evil for reasons of caprice. Rather, his forbiddance was expression of his goodness—another occasion of paternal protection: "In the day that you eat of it you shall surely die."

THE GENEROSITY OF DIVINE WELCOME

What's clear from Genesis 1–2 is that God had readied a world for welcome. *Homemaking*, as a word to describe God's labor on behalf of humanity, conveys the sense of God's mindfulness toward the man and the woman he greets at the door. The creation stories of Genesis 1–2 affirm our first improbable gift of grace: divine hospitality. The home that God made wasn't his greatest ambition; the guests were. And if the search for home is fundamental to every human longing and *homesickness* is a way of characterizing every human disappointment, Genesis 1–2 teaches us why. There was once a place for everything, and everything in its place. We were meant to be taken in.

The creation accounts in Genesis differ dramatically from other creation myths, which read like war tales, depicting a violent beginning to the cosmos. The *Enuma Elish*, an ancient Babylonian creation myth, tells the story of Marduk, a god who aspires to supremacy in the pantheon of Babylonian gods. He promises to fight and defeat Tiamat, the watery chaos, if he will be recognized king of the universe. In the Aztec creation story two gods pull the earth goddess down from the sky, ripping her into two pieces to form the heavens and the earth. Because she is angry at the violence done to her, she demands sacrifices of human blood. In the ancient Greek creation stories, there are intrigues of murder, incest, rape, and cannibalism. The gods beget other gods, and their petty jealousies provoke internecine fighting in the heavenly realms. In the ancient Assyrian myths the gods of the sky, storms, earth, sun, and water, having made the land and the sea and feeling bored after the effort, wondered what else needed to be done. They determined that humans would be useful for the tasks of tilling the land and celebrating the religious festivals, so the gods commissioned them with these tasks as well as with transmission of the creation story.

Much has been made of the overlap between the Genesis story and other ancient creation myths, but it must also be noted how terrifically different the stories are. The Genesis creation depicts no violent struggle of good and evil, no celestial war between the gods. The narrative doesn't hang in suspense, as if we're left speculating as to who might prevail over the chaos. Rather, there is a God who denudes the darkness with the sound of his voice, and his authority and love are absolute. At his command, the universe illuminates, and the earth and skies and seas teem with life. Everything obeys him—and this obedience, demanded of humans, ensures not simply God's happiness but their own flourishing. *And God blessed them.*

The biblical account does not deny that we owe to the Maker of heaven and earth our reverent worship, but neither does it affirm that our worth is equivalent to our subservience. God has not created humans to serve his capricious whim. In the *Dictionary of Creation Myths*, scholars David and Margaret Leeming note some of the similarities and differences between the *Enuma Elish* and the Genesis creation accounts. "As in the Enuma Elish, humans in Genesis are created from clay, and man works for God. He tends the garden and names the plants and animals, but unlike in the Enuma Elish, God creates a paradise specifically for man, has a relationship with him, and treats him *as a kind of god.*"[16]

Yahweh (of Genesis 1) and Elohim (of Genesis 2) grant dignity to the human beings he creates. The Creator God serves his creation by sheltering them in the beauty of a garden and the radiant light of his presence. He makes them a home.

Our oldest record of God's homemaking is not the book of Genesis, however; for this, we must read the book of Job, where God defends himself against Job's accusations of cruel indifference by citing his homemaking and housekeeping. The Almighty claims divine parentage over all of creation, and the world is pictured as having been birthed by God's labor and as bearing proof of God's paternity (Job 38:28-29). The book of Job uses many other domestic images to convey God's creative acts: God is the tradesman, who pours a foundation, determines measurements, and lays a cornerstone (Job 38:4-7). God is the estate manager who walks the length and breadth of his land and keeps inventory of the storehouses (Job 38:16-24). God is the principal shepherd, exercising control over the stars as if they are animals to herd (Job 38:31-33). Though there is scientific rationality to the created order, the universe isn't pictured mechanistically; in the book of Job creation is home and estate, art and craft.

In her book *Getting Involved with God,* Ellen Davis discusses the theological vision presented in these final chapters of the book of Job as centered less on God's moral character (as we think of it) and more on his "aesthetic preferences"—which Annie Dillard calls "pizzazz."[17] "Love of pizzazz," writes Davis, "is compatible with an aspect of God's moral character with which we are familiar: God's self-giving generosity. What God shows Job is the highest form of causality operative in the universe, the generosity that brings another into free being."[18] The generosity to which Davis refers, the generosity to which Job and Genesis testify, is the generosity of homemaking.

THE GOOD NEWS OF ADOPTION

Several months ago the clock blared its quotidian 5 a.m. alarm. Bleary-eyed, I shuffled downstairs for my morning cup of coffee, and in the kitchen, flipped on the lights. I came instantly awake. The kitchen window, tall and wide enough for a human body, was cranked open. The blinds had been jerked up, the screen hastily removed. Someone was in the house.

I ran upstairs to check the children's bedrooms and found their beds warm and occupied. *Thank God.* Then I woke Ryan, shaking him by the shoulder and whispering urgently, "Someone's in the house. The kitchen window was forced open." He was up instantly, pulling on pants and simultaneously descending the stairs. Together, we tread through the house on tiptoe, opening closet doors, flooding each room with light. But we found no intruder.

"You're lucky," the policeman said when he arrived later that morning to file a report. When he had dusted the windowsill, the faint outline of a man's thick-soled work boot had appeared, but he could find no footprint inside the house. "The intruder might have shone his flashlight around and decided there wasn't much worth taking. Or maybe he heard you coming down the stairs early this morning and took off." It wasn't a break-in, at least not quite, he said. But it still left me with a sense of invasion and a shudder of fear.

There is someone in the house. Humanity's first home fell prey to burglary the day a snake slithered into a garden—and the children opened wide the door to let him in. Post-Genesis 3, we are not safe; we are not at rest. As C. S. Lewis suggests, the world is "enemy-occupied territory."[19] And rather than dedicating our lives to the worship and obedience of God as God had intended, we have been inconsiderate house guests, too self-preoccupied for keeping company with our generous Father and Host.

To be sure, the first Maker of home might have easily cast us out and prevented return. God might have given to his recalcitrant children the strange names of the prophet's first daughter and son: "No Mercy" and "Not My People" (Hos 1:6, 9). And yet the God of the Bible is not unrelenting in anger, for time and again he lays down severity for the sake of mercy. Though he grieves the sin of his people and judges it, he yet designs a way to spare them his justified wrath.

> How can I give you up, O Ephraim?
>> How can I hand you over, O Israel?
> How can I make you like Admah?
>> How can I treat you like Zeboiim?
> My heart recoils within me;
>> my compassion grows warm and tender.
> I will not execute my burning anger. (Hos 11:8-9)

Through the atoning sacrifice of Jesus Christ, our slow-to-anger, compassionate God makes a way back home. As the Scriptures teach us to hope, God will one day clean house and restore the earth to a greater glory than Eden. Just as we were put in a garden, taken in by the love of the homemaking God, we will one day be put in a city—and welcomed back.

But our hope for home isn't only future. If, in the beginning, the Father made a home for his children, in the fullness of time, he has chosen to welcome back the prodigal, restoring to his penitent children their full inheritance. This is the New Testament good news of adoption. Home isn't yet fully restored to humanity, but humanity, through the sonship of Jesus, our faithful elder brother, is restored to the family of God. On the cross the enemies of home—snake, sin, death—were defeated and their sting removed. All who look up at that work of divine mercy receive their welcome and the promise of eventual home.

When the prodigal returns from the far country in Jesus' most famous parable, his father embraces him despite that he'd voluntarily left home and effectively cut all ties with the family. The son, however, does not presume upon family privilege when he slinks back to the family he has betrayed. He reckons his best hope lay in working for pay. "I am no longer worthy to be called your son," he intends to confess. "Treat me as one of your hired servants" (Lk 15:19). Nevertheless, the father will not suffer that prepared speech. Instead, he kisses his lost son, demonstrating publicly their reconciliation and his son's restoration. As Thomas Oden describes in his systematic theology, "The prodigal was not merely pardoned, but to his astonishment received back into the family with full rights of sonship. Remission of sin is followed by the reconciling embrace of the Father. Justification is not merely a cold announcement of nonliability, but a warm welcome from the waiting Father."[20] The prodigal is not merely acquitted: he is taken back in. This is the good news of home as the gospel tells it.

Adoption, as an important doctrine of the New Testament, speaks to the reconciling love of the Father. It also reminds us of the reality of sin and the necessity of grace. For though we might have once been God's children by virtue of birth, we are now only children by virtue of adoption. We cannot presume upon our welcome home; it has been offered at great cost to the Father. "Conscience amid modernity has become so seared that we imagine we are welcomed by God precisely while we are doing what God condemns," writes Oden, in summary of Reinhold Niebuhr's thought.[21] One great heresy of home is that there is any other way to enter but through repentance and faith in Jesus Christ. To come home is, at the very least, to admit the reasons for having left and to acknowledge the leaving as offense.

Opening the refrigerator in our homes today, we are thrown into sudden panic. The GladWare leaks, and the shelves are sticky.

In the dark of this day's morning, we find the window of the kitchen standing open: someone is in the house. But the good news of Genesis—and the great news of the gospel—is that someone is indeed taking care. He will banish the intruder, and he will restore beauty and order to the house, his sons and daughters to the family. The primordial Homemaker is an adoptive Father, and his empathetic homemaking will last throughout eternity.

In our forever home, the lights never go out.

BORDER CROSSINGS

On (Not) Staying Put

**151 GLENDON AVENUE
TORONTO, ONTARIO**

I SLICE KALE INTO THE SOUP. Ribbons fall into the roiling boil and turn a brilliant emerald green. It's Saturday, and we have just returned home from our favorite farmers' market at Toronto's Evergreen Brick Works, our arms laden with many-hued berries and lettuces. In the summer the market is fat and fertile, plump and red like the tomatoes. The Niagara orchards yield proud sweet peaches, the Ontario fields sweet juicy corn. Nevertheless, the worm is reserved for the market's early birds; both peaches and corn will have disappeared from the market stalls by 10 a.m. in August.

The Brick Works has become our family's regular Saturday morning destination, though not just for the purpose of filling our bags with Ontario's bounty. We make it an excuse to eat beignets and climb the gravel paths up to the rim of the valley, where we catch our favorite view of the place we call home. The kids scramble on large rocks, watching the seasons as they change. Spring robes; fall flames. Eventually, their perch affords them full view of winter's nakedness. The skyscrapers, unlike the valley, stand impervious to the weather.

This valley's shale and clay had once been dedicated to building Toronto's skyline, but when the Don Valley Brick Works closed in 1984 and the kilns cooled, the buildings were abandoned and the landscape was left scarred by industrialization. In the mid-1990s, however, six million dollars were raised to rehabilitate the land. Twenty years later Toronto's Evergreen Brickworks has recently been named a top ten finalist in the National Geographic Geotourism Challenge. It lies in the heart of Toronto's ravines, which, as one author put it, are akin to Venice's canals and San Francisco's hills: "They are the heart of the city's emotional geography."[1]

I confess to feeling emotional about this place, though I'm not a Toronto native. Whenever we host out-of-town guests, we bring them to the Brick Works, knowing this land and the rehabilitated buildings, scrawled with graffiti, best represent the environmental, artistic, and philanthropic ethos of the city. (To boot, they'll like the food.) Similar to the High Line on Manhattan's West Side, the Brick Works embodies a unique urban beauty. As James Corner, the landscape architect for the High Line project, has explained, projects like these are "irreproducible anywhere else without significant loss of origin and locality."[2] Their beauty is not imported but organic; it simply can't be transplanted.

Though people easily can.

OUR DESIRE FOR ROOTEDNESS

Before Seattle resident Edith Macefield died at age eighty-six in 2008, she refused to sell her house to developers for the $1 million they had purportedly offered. Macefield wanted to die at home.

Seven years later, long after Macefield's death, the small six-hundred-square-foot bungalow continued to crouch low in the middle of high-rise commercial buildings in Seattle's Ballard neighborhood. The house stood as a symbol of an earlier generation's simplicity, stability, and rootedness. It even became something of a shrine to welcome pilgrims like Elizabeth Forte, who had brought her three young children to pay homage to Macefield's legacy.

"It's interesting what it makes you feel," said Forte in an interview with the *New York Times*.[3] "Our generation is constantly moving and looking for something new, but your parents stayed put." As proof that this desire for rootedness has taken root in the consciousness of neighborhood residents, "A local tattoo parlor has inked a likeness of the home—along with the word 'steadfastness'—on a number of people's bodies."[4]

It is neither strange that people would derive such deep connection to the house of a practical stranger nor that they would wish to ink their bodies in tribute. (Seattle residents have also launched the Macefield Music Festival and begun serving a rye-based cocktail, the Edith Macefield, at local bars.) To lose the place that bore witness to Macefield's life was to lay mortality bare. A body reduced to dust and a house reduced to debris: in the rubble would lie humanity's illusory claim to permanence. Yes, there was much to preserve in preserving a small house. In keeping something in place.

To speak of place is to presuppose the body. There is, as theologian Craig Bartholomew has insisted, an "inevitable logic" between emplacement and embodiment. In other words, to consider the Genesis account, in order for God to "put" our human parents in a garden, they needed bodies. Lacking corporality, we cannot be put anywhere. When the first human was formed, the Lord stooped to the ground and scooped together a pile of dust, expiring his breath into the soil and bringing forth life. Adam's name bears out the connection he has to the land. (*Adama*, in Hebrew, means "cultivable ground.") As the Genesis account illustrates, we owe our bodies to the earth. We need place to flourish.

ADDRESS HISTORY

Because God made a material world for material beings, calling it very good, home—if we are to mean the word in its most biblical sense—must be a *place*. Place was one of God's first gifts to his people. And as the apostle Paul explains to the men of Athens gathered in the Areopagus, each place in our lives is a holy site: "He made from one man every nation of mankind to live on all the face of the earth, having determined allotted periods and boundaries of their dwelling place, that they should seek God, and perhaps feel their way toward him and find him" (Acts 17:26-27). No place is insignificant in our stories. In fact, in paying them attention, we pay attention to the salvific movement of God. Wherever we move, we may be sure of this: God always moves us toward himself.

An address history bears important witness to the God in whom we live and move and have our being (Acts 17:28). Nevertheless, many of us live disconnected from place. Despite our massive carbon footprint, we live, as it were, lightly on the land, paying too little attention to our relationship with place. Social media encourages us to cultivate virtual lives and loves, often at the expense of responsibilities that are most proximate.

Technology has granted us the *telegraph* (writing over distance), the *telephone* (sound over distance) and *television* (sight over distance), as well as the miracles of Skype and FaceTime, which provide the illusion of presence over distance. As an almost technological inevitability, the twenty-first-century North American is distanced from place.[5]

No wonder we fail to share one of the central preoccupations of the Old and New Testaments: geography. In the story of Jacob, which we'll explore in further detail at the end of the chapter, the names of places are critically important. After leaving Canaan to flee his twin brother's vengeance, Jacob spends twenty years in Haran with his uncle and eventual father-in-law, Laban. When he returns to Canaan, Genesis details three specific places of sojourn for Jacob and his family (Gen 33:18; 35:1, 27). First, Shechem. Jacob and his family settle among foreigners, and his daughter, Dinah, is sexually assaulted, held hostage by the man who will pay however great a bride price to make her his wife. Not only is Dinah defiled but the entire village of Shechem is plundered in revenge by the sons of Jacob, who will not stand for their sister to be treated like a prostitute.

Next, God bids Jacob to leave Shechem and return to Bethel. The stone he had, more than two decades earlier, improvised as a pillow and set up as a pillar to God, is used to build a rightful altar of worship and Jacob's name change—from Jacob to Israel—is reprised. Finally, Jacob returns to his father Isaac in Southern Canaan, in Hebron, to presumably stay until the family must flee when famine strikes.

Shechem, Bethel, and Hebron may be meaningless names to modern readers, but they are not insignificant dots on a map. Rather, they trace Abraham's initial journey into the land (Gen 12), as well as the first sites of the Canaanite conquest (Josh 8; 10). John Sailhamer notes,

This is to show that the conquest of the land had already been accomplished in a symbolic way in the times of the fathers, demonstrated by means of their building their altars and purchasing property. Thus it shows that in the deeds of the fathers there is a source of trust that the Lord has cared for them from the very start and that he will still remain trustworthy in the days of the descendants of the fathers later on.[6]

Jacob's address history points back to the promises given to Abraham, if also ahead to the inheritance of Israel.

As the apostle Paul has formulated it, the arc of our stories can be traced according to two important markers: time and terrain, "periods and boundaries." In part, to *place*. But how often do we hear faith stories as place stories? It seems easier to talk about our lives according to its various seasons: a rebellious adolescence, the first year of motherhood, a period of illness. We moderns are exactingly attuned to time, but we are not carefully attuned to place.

OUR HABITS OF MOBILITY

No doubt this disconnect from place is partially owed to the mobility of modern life. It is hardly extraordinary for Americans to move multiple times, even within the span of a year. But lest it seem that earlier generations were more geographically stable than people today, some research reveals otherwise. According to data reported by the US Census Bureau, the average American will move 11.7 times in their lifetime (and most frequently between the ages of eighteen and forty-five). That will seem like a significantly high figure except that it represents a decrease from decades past. As the Federal Reserve Board concluded in a 2013 paper, "The interstate migration rate in 2011 was 53 percent below its 1948-1971 average, while the rates of moving between counties within the same state and of moving within the same county fell 44 and 36 percent, respectively, over the same period."[7] Within the United States, economists are noting that occupational mobility is on the decline. And because people are changing jobs less frequently, which might have otherwise provided a reason for relocating, they seem to prefer staying put. (By global comparison, however, US citizens, along with citizens from New Zealand, Finland, and Norway, rank as the most mobile in the world, with the exception of those fleeing crisis).

There will be debate, according to the data, about our relative mobility. Nevertheless, many, like me, have known the grief of transience and the longing for stability. Though we've gotten good at packing and unpacking the boxes and making fast friends, this life of constant change has wearied us. Instinctively, we know that place will not be cheated—that a superficial life is rooted shallowly. To stay in place is to grow and deepen a life; leaving is a violence. It's important to note that theologian Walter Brueggemann has called our biggest existential crisis today not meaninglessness but *rootlessness*. In his book *The Land*, he describes the human longing for stability. To flourish, humans need *place*. "There are no meanings apart from roots," Brueggemann concludes.[8] When humans become geographically unmoored, either voluntarily or involuntarily, they put themselves at risk of losing not just connection to their history and its people, but recognition of themselves.

James Wood discovered the peril of displacement when he moved from London to Boston. In his essay for the *London Review of Books* titled "On Not Going Home," Wood, Harvard professor of the practice of literary criticism, describes feeling alienated from his birthplace as well as his place of residence. Though he's lived in the United States for eighteen years, despite all his practical familiarity with his Boston neighborhood, he can't shake his sense of estrangement. There is, as he explains, "no comprehension, no real connection, no past, despite all the years I have lived there—just a tugging distance from it all." It's as if, in Wood's words, "a light veil of alienation [has been] thrown over everything." Yet even when Wood returns to England, the veil remains. "There's a quality of masquerade when I return, as if I were putting on my wedding suit, to see if it still fits." Only now does Wood understand that life was irrevocably altered the day he crossed the ocean.[9] Uprooted trees can be transplanted, but this isn't to say they become indigenous species.

As a young man Jonathan Wilson-Hartgrove imagined himself more broad-minded than his rural neighbors. He left the South and put his American passport to work for God, but the travel eventually wrung him out. In his book *The Wisdom of Stability*, Wilson-Hartgrove describes having "stumbled into a little intentional community of Christians [in Iraq] who were trying to love one another and their neighbors."[10] There, Wilson-Hartgrove discovered the beauty of St. Benedict's call to stability, and when he returned to the States, he and his wife founded an intentional community called Rutba. They vowed stability in Walltown, North Carolina, an urban community struggling with issues of violence, poverty, and despair. No matter what happened, they promised to stay.

FORCED MIGRATION

It is a worthy investment of a lifetime to vow stability to a place, and I envy friends and family, like my brother-in-law and sister-in-law living in Chicago's West Side, whose deep, lasting investment to a community is yielding the fruit of faithful presence across years. Stability embraces God's good gift of place, and it is one important practice of home. Nevertheless, there are countless examples of the impossibilities of stability. Not everyone, like my husband and me or James Wood, has drunk the bold wine of modern freedom and chosen mobility at whim. Sometimes leaving a place is the only safe alternative to the jeopardy of staying put. Somehow we must find God in those stories too.

In *The Warmth of Other Suns: The Epic Story of American's Great Migration*, Isabel Wilkerson traces the history of the six million African Americans who left the American South between 1915 and 1970, yearning to find freedom and hope in cities like New York, Chicago, and Los Angeles.

In her book Wilkerson introduces us to three African Americans who left the South during the Great Migration. Robert Joseph Pershing Foster left Louisiana for Los Angeles, arriving after a harrowing trip across the desert during which he was refused lodging. In California Foster became a successful surgeon. Ida Mae Brandon Gladney left Mississippi for Chicago, living into her nineties with her Southern drawl and watching the demise of her Chicago neighborhood from her front picture window. George Swanson Sterling left Florida for New York City, where his children tragically succumbed to the corruption of the city.

Robert, Ida, and George's acts of leaving may not have scripted the fairy-tale endings they had hoped for, but as Wilkerson's book describes, none could have entertained the fantasy of staying put. Robert couldn't freely practice medicine in the South, though he had proved his professional distinction as a doctor during World War II. Ida Mae and her husband left the injustice of the sharecropping system, where fewer than one out of five sharecroppers saw a profit at the end of the year. George fled a lynching. In many respects these three people were escaping the South for freedom and the sake of their own humanity. What's perhaps most startling about the Great Migration is that the movement "had more in common with the vast movements of refugees of famine, war, and genocide in other parts of the world."[11] African Americans left the South in droves, traveling far and braving danger, not simply because they wanted a change of scenery. They needed an alternative to death.

Not all of us can be commended to stay in place. In fact, leaving may be our only hope. When war ignites, when famine desiccates, when disease ravages a landscape, when injustice can no longer be tolerated, people are forced from their home without warning and without choice, instabilities beyond their control seizing from them their land and their sense of belonging. Home is amputated, and people become placeless. This may be, as Marilynne Robinson describes "as inevitable and irreversible as the drift of continents," but it is also "full of disruption and grief and regret."[12] Surely one evidence of the world's fallenness from grace is its failure to provide stability. To lose our places is to lose our place.

It is to this grief of the loss of place that the gospel of a home-making God speaks, and stability is part of the eternal hope for the people of God. If we are strangers and aliens now, carrying estrangement as our oldest habit, we are destined for a better country, a city prepared by God himself—a *home*.[13] And not only will this unpredictable, unstable world be remade, regaining its original stability; we can also enjoy a present-tense hope. Even now there is a God who meets us at every border. He is a God who gives meaning, not just to the periods of our lives but to the boundaries of our dwellings.

As Jacob came to understand, he is not just God of heaven; he is also God of every liminal place.

JACOB'S FIRST BORDER CROSSING: BETHEL

Abraham's grandson, Jacob, is a case study in instability. In many of the biblical episodes of Jacob's life, we find him in an in-between place. In his commentary on Genesis, Hebrew scholar Robert Alter notes, "Jacob is represented as a border crosser, a man of liminal experiences."[14] And as Jonathan Wilson-Hartgrove claims,

> You'd be hard pressed to find a worse model of stability than Jacob. As people whose impulses are shaped by an epoch of hyper mobility, we may indeed find a true father in Jacob. We are, after all, a people on the run, propelled forward both by the ambition that keeps our eyes on the horizon and the broken relationships that we try leaving behind.[15]

There is recognizable instability and sinful fragmentation in Jacob's journeying, and his days end not in Canaan but Egypt. Jacob's life is characterized by flight (see Gen 28:10-22).

In the first important scene of Jacob's on-the-run life, Jacob is being sent away by Isaac to find a wife in Paddan-aram, the land of patrimony.[16] Jacob's departure is so urgent (because Esau is determined to kill him for his betrayal) that there is no time to pack provisions, and his odds of return seem unlikely, except that his father, Isaac, reaffirms the promises God gave to his grandfather: "May he give the blessing of Abraham to you." Readers of the biblical narrative will remember a similar scene in Genesis 24, where Abraham sends his servant back to Haran to find a wife for Isaac—and understand that not all instability is initially voluntary. Sometimes we inherit our "placelessness" from our mothers and fathers, our grandmothers and grandfathers.

As Jacob journeyed from Canaan to Paddan-aram, the text records that he "came to a certain place." The only particularity of this place—*maqom*—is its anonymity. In fact, its geographical indistinctiveness is emphasized six times in the short passage: this "place" was neither origin nor destination. It was a way station in Jacob's journey and might easily have been ignored.

Except that Bethel is Jacob's place of divine vision. As sleep descends, he dreams a strange vision of a ladder (or something similar to the flight of steps ascending the Mesopotamian ziggurat) on which the angels of God ascend and descend. The voice of God thunders with the Abrahamic promise, and on oath, promises Jacob's return. The promise of return is, of course, an implicit promise of stability. However, as Wilson-Hartgrove notes, it is not Jacob who vows to his own stability but God. "There it is," writes Wilson-Hartgrove, "stability as pure gift. God meets Jacob when he is a homeless scoundrel on the run and says, 'I love you. I want you. I will make this a place for you, and I will meet you here.'. . . [Similarly] God offers us stability in the only thing that cannot fail—God's faithfulness itself."[17] Under a moonless sky, a placeless man gains hope, a nameless place, a name. The *place* becomes Bethel, the "house of God."

Bethel reveals that God is present in every liminal place, lending his anchoring weight to our weightless lives. Our in-between places—between jobs, between cities, between houses—can easily feel like a bookmark, as if their only job was separating past from future. But these places are indeed part of the story, even when we have failed to give them a name. And most peculiarly, a generic, in-between place can even become a temple in the desert—a *house of God*. A nameless place can be the site of tentatively taking our first step toward trust; it's at Bethel that we can begin believing in a God, who journeys with us.

JACOB'S SECOND BORDER CROSSING: GILEAD

In the second scene of Jacob's on-the-run life, we find him fleeing his uncle, Laban (see Gen 31). Jacob has spent twenty years away from Canaan, and in Paddan-aram he has greatly prospered. Jacob's wealth, however, does not change the reality that the cheater has himself been cheated: Jacob has worked for his uncle for two decades and earned no consistent wage. Worse, Laban's sons bear him reproach for his financial success.

Though an outsider might describe Jacob's time in Paddan-aram as fruitful and blessed, Jacob characterizes his twenty-year sojourn as "suffering and toil."[18] For despite having been initially embraced by Laban, upon arrival, as "my bone and my flesh" and marrying into the family, Jacob remained for two decades an outsider. Even Laban's daughters felt they had been cruelly treated by their father: "Do we still have any share in the inheritance of our father's house? Why, we have been counted by him as strangers for he has sold us, and he has wholly consumed our money."[19] As Robert Alter explains,

> In a socially decorous marriage, a large part of the bride-price would go to the bride. Laban, who first appeared in the narrative (chapter 24) eyeing the possible profit to himself in a betrothal transaction, has evidently pocketed all the fruits of Jacob's fourteen years of labor. His daughters thus see themselves reduced to chattel by their father, not married off but rather sold for profit, as though they were not his flesh and blood.[20]

Laban has never considered Jacob a son, and in mishandling the bride price Jacob paid for his daughters, he has also estranged Leah and Rachel. In Paddan-aram it becomes clear that years don't always make for a home. Even bloodlines can prove too fragile a tie of belonging. We can't make home of every place we land.

If Paddan-aram isn't home, Canaan is. "Then the LORD said to Jacob, 'Return to the land of your fathers and to your kindred, and I will be with you.'" This understanding of home, which God imposes on Jacob, stands in contrast to the self-understanding of Abraham when he sends his servant back to Haran in search of Isaac's wife, instructing him to "go to *my* country and to *my* kindred." Abraham seems to have been tethered to his ancestral past in ways that Jacob was not. Perhaps like many immigrants, Abraham grew increasingly nostalgic about the land he had left as a young man, fondness a product of his old age.

Taking a three-day lead ahead of Laban and his men, Jacob is finally overtaken by Laban, whose greeting underscores Jacob's changed geographical fealty. "And now you have gone away because you longed greatly for *your father's house.*" Despite the more than twenty years Jacob has lived with Laban in Haran, despite his ancestors' lived history in that place, Jacob pined noticeably for return to Canaan. The rupture between the "old country" and "new country" was complete in Jacob's lifetime. Perhaps this new loyalty is most fully evidenced in the treaty Laban and Jacob finally declare as they heap up stones as evidence of peace. "Laban called it Jegar-sahadutha, but Jacob called it Galeed." Laban speaks Aramaic, the language of the old country. Jacob speaks Hebrew, the language of the new.

JACOB'S THIRD BORDER CROSSING: JABBOK

Genesis 32 features Jacob's return into the land of Canaan, where he must face a reunion with his brother, Esau. Will he find that Esau's anger has cooled? Or will Esau, having stoked the fires of revenge in Jacob's prolonged absence, make good on his former promise to kill his brother? For Jacob, as for many of us, the sense of internal displacement is not only owed to geographical dislocation. We are not only estranged from our place: we are estranged from the people we once shared close relationship with, the people most responsible for loving us and taking us in. Belonging has been strangled by bitterness, and if ever we are to find our way home, we will have to find and follow paths of repentance and forgiveness.

Jacob sends ahead messengers, who return with reports that Esau advances with four hundred men, the "standard number for a regiment or raiding party."[21] It does not look like peace but war. Jacob scurries to send gifts. He flings prayer to the sky. He sends everyone across a stream called Jabbok, remaining to wrestle his fear alone. Bless me, he demands of the strange angelic messenger. In one sense Jacob emerges victorious from the wrestling match: he is blessed, deserving now of a new name, Israel. In another sense Jacob is vanquished: he is wounded, having his hip put out of joint by the wilderness stranger. But the site of dislocation is also the site of theophany: "I have seen God face to face." Twenty years have prospered Jacob, and while they haven't *emplaced* him, they have *enfaithed* him.

Bethel, Gilead, Jabbok: these are the liminal places of the narrative, and they provide consolation for our seemingly aimless lives. The all-present God of Jacob keeps company wherever we are. God is stable, even when we are not.

A STABLE HOPE

In the Benedictine order, novices are asked to take three lifelong vows: to stability, to fidelity, and to obedience. The monks pledge their loyalty to Christ and to an obedient lifetime in the same place with the same people—"without weakening or seeking escape."[22] Novices promise, despite the odds, to stay. Understanding the inherent difficulties of stability, Benedict explained that any newcomer to the monastery must be left at the door, knocking four or five days. If he persisted, he would be allowed entry, but only after being warned of the difficulties and hardships of this path of chosen devotion to God. After two months, if the newcomer maintained his desire to stay, he would be read the entire Rule. After six months, if he still pledged himself to the monastic life, he would be tested again. Four months later the process would be repeated. If, more than a year later, after repeated warnings of hardship and multiple readings of the Rule, the newcomer wanted to take his vows, he could announce his intentions before the community and lay his written promise on the altar. Only then was he accepted. Benedict made the process of promising permanence deliberately arduous—equally arduous to the difficult and often counter-intuitive work of staying put.

Staying put is a fast from our appetite for constant change. Benedict knew it would feel nearly impossible at times to abide the monotony of staying in one place, not to mention the weariness of entertaining the same company. He knew that stability would challenge the instinctive blame we lay at the feet of our circumstances and expose the false hope of scenery change. Though Benedict might have admitted the legitimate call of God on a person's life to travel to the ends of the earth preaching the good news, he also understood the quiet courage required for steadfastness and staying.

"Don't easily leave your place," advised Abba Antony.[23]

Stability is good advice, but sometimes, like Jacob, we end up with a life that, in the rearview mirror, looks much more erratic than we might had originally intended. The greatest consolation for the geographically displaced is not Jacob but Jesus: the Son of God was himself a border crosser. He left home and its happiness with abandon, even delight. As the Gospel of John describes, Jesus Christ left his Father's side in heaven and came into a world that he himself made but where people received him as a stranger (Jn 1:11). The Creator became the Christ, condescending to rescue those alienated from home and its Maker.

God has shared the human sorrow of losing place. Crucified under Pontius Pilate, Jesus died the death of a criminal, becoming the sacrificial lamb who suffered "outside the camp" (Heb 13:12-13). He knew the near intolerable pain of outsiderdom. And his forsakenness is our fortune.

By faith in the God of Jacob and the God and Father of our Lord Jesus Christ, we are carried through the middle act in which God names the liminal places—and also names us. He promises home to all of humanity's tent dwellers.

We might not stay put. But we are never lost.

5

PERISHED THINGS
And Imperishable Home

707 MAE AVENUE
KENT, OHIO

I AM A PIG-TAILED SEVEN-YEAR-OLD with a knack for spelling. Sometimes Mrs. Lee, my chocolate-skinned teacher, asks me to circulate to other tables, offering help. I like that responsibility. But most of all, I like disappearing inside the antique bathtub that hulks at the center of the classroom, serving as a reading corner and a grand porcelain invitation to finish math quickly. Under the blankets I burrow in books. When the final school bell rings, my brother and I begin walking the eight blocks home from Holden Elementary School at the same moment my mother wakes behind the drawn curtains of our red, rented bungalow and shakes off the bone-weariness of her hospital night shift. Twenty minutes later, the metal side door bangs open. "We're home!" Groggily, Mom greets us in the kitchen.

We moved from Missouri to Ohio in order for my father to finish coursework for his doctoral program. My mother worked nights to pay the rent on our small two-bedroom house, slept days while my brother and I attended school. We lived in Kent one year before we moved to Tennessee. Before the summer of 2014, I hadn't been back since 1980.

I returned when I began trying to fill the holes of our family story. I needed, for the purposes of this book, to tread the sites of memory before trying to puzzle together their meaning. My children, my mother, and I committed two weeks to the road. We set out to find three of my childhood homes as well as to visit some of the schools and churches I had attended.

On the last Saturday in June, I piled six of us in the minivan, left Toronto and met my mother in Kent (and Mrs. Lee, now gray and crinkly-eyed) before driving through Kentucky's bluegrass hills on our way to Jefferson City, Tennessee, a small mining town near the Smoky Mountains. Eventually, we headed across the state to Jackson, where my father had been a communications professor at Union University. The kids endured the hundreds of miles by listening to nearly all of the Harry Potter series as I searched for the "narrative order" that David Brooks mentions in his column "Going Home Again."[1] Each of these three places represented our family before the common era of loss: the premature deaths of my father, at forty-nine, and my brother, at twenty-four. In truth, I went home to reclaim the perished things.

Weeks before the trip I called my mother to ask if my father had finished writing his dissertation. Wanting to pick up a copy when we were in Kent, I had just spent a half hour on the phone with a student clerk in what I imagined to be the dusty basement of the Kent State University library. He combed through what I imagined to be the microfiche. Mike Pollock. Michael Kent Pollock. Michael K. Pollock. I had asked the clerk to search every conceivable name the dissertation might be filed under, but it wasn't found.

"Did he finish? Did he turn it in?" I asked Mom over the phone, my voice rising with shrill accusation, stunned at her carelessness with memory.

For better, for worse, we speak little of my father now. As I have come to learn, there is no one to teach you to suffer loss. Grief is an improvised art. There are no rules to decide upon; there is no form for imitation. When my father died, my mother and I learned to agree mostly on the decorum of silence—with the exception of one tearful phone conversation from my college dormitory room, when I had stretched the corded telephone into the bathroom and heaved up sobs from the tile floor, finding her voice warmed by compassion. In the months, then years, that followed what I want to clinically call "the events," the earth opened and a gulf swallowed my father (and later, my brother) whole. The perished things disappeared, and we stood mute over the fissure.

"I don't know, Jen. I can't remember that far back."

732 LAKEWOOD DRIVE
JEFFERSON CITY, TENNESSEE

I SKID OUT OF CONTROL, lose control of the handlebars, and plunge headfirst into the gravel. Bloodied, I soldier up the hill. "What happened?" my mother asks with visible concern when she greets me at the door. She scurries for iodine and

Band-Aids. She is most reliable in these moments, and as a little girl I am glad to find her home.

But home isn't central to my memory of this place: Carson Newman College, where both of my parents worked, is. After school the bus dropped my brother and me in front of the college infirmary. Until dinnertime, when we warmed leftovers and ate silently in the infirmary kitchen with my mother before she finished her shift, my brother and I shirked the shadow of boredom. We raced on the infirmary crutches until our underarms rubbed raw. We spied on the occasional student sleeping in one of the back bedrooms, musing about the terrifying (if also deliciously adult) ailment called "the kissing disease." From the display in the lobby we stole informational pamphlets on STDs. When all else failed, we wandered over to the student union with a few shiny coins to buy Tab and cinnamon-sugar doughnuts. The afternoon often ended with a couple of improvised games of pool.

On a summer day in 2014 I try the heavy-hinged screen door of the infirmary, and it groans open to a carpeted foyer, linoleum corridors, and the familiar antiseptic smell of three years of company keeping with the brother I had occasionally denied our relation to. At eighteen I went away to college; at twenty-two, I married. And using geographic distance as reasonable excuse for failing to call, I didn't talk frequently to my brother—until his psychotic break. After anxious days without word, we finally found David in a local hospital from which he made paranoid calls, alluding to conspiratorial threats on his life. He survived this fright. Righted himself like a near-sunken ship. Months of stability. Then death by his own hand. Which I don't suppose anyone knows to expect.

Regret in death is not undone. Perished things, like millstones, can sink without struggle or sound. Death can be noiseless. Especially from two states away.

After our visit to the infirmary, we cross the street to find the building that had housed my father's first office. But instead of finding the building deserted, as we expected, we have chance acquaintance with the departmental secretary who'd been hired the year after my dad left. "Of course!" she exclaims. "Mike Pollock. He left right before I arrived." She springs from her chair and yanks yearbooks from the shelves, consulting the index and flipping pages to find him wearing a wide, plaid tie. "Let me give you the number of Dr. Walton, who taught with your father in the department," she offers. "He's still in the area, and I'm sure he'd love to hear from you!" Minutes later, I introduce myself, trembling: *Jen Pollock Michel, back to visit some of my childhood homes.* John describes my father warmly as "creative" and "tender," fondly remembering a theater production the two of them performed together.

In the hallway, tears fall on the perished things. Only fools say time heals.

In Marilynne Robinson's first novel, *Housekeeping*, Ruth and Lucille have been serially abandoned by the suicide of their mother, then by the death of their grandmother, and finally because of the unwillingness of two older relatives to care for them. Their mother's younger sister, Sylvie, a vagrant with a history of mental instability, returns to the town of Fingerbone to assume their supervision.

The town of Fingerbone sits on the edge of a lake, which has claimed a number of lives, including Ruth and Lucille's grandfather and the other passengers of the train that plunged, years earlier, off the trestle and sank to the bottom. The narrator, Ruth, wonders what would be recovered if the lake were dredged. "There would be a general reclaiming of fallen buttons and misplaced spectacles, of neighbors and kin, till time and error and accident were undone, and the world made comprehensible and whole."[2] There, at the bottom at the lake, they would recover the perished things. Sense would be made of the fragility of life. The loss of home would be accounted for, a more permanent hope found.

This two-week road trip is that kind of excavation. I unearth the past like a lost button—my father and brother like two pairs of broken glasses.

156 CHARJEAN DRIVE
JACKSON, TENNESSEE

PENNED IN THE BACKYARD is our pit bull, Tiger. Next door live the Lyndon children, Jeffrey and Samantha, who we play with only when we've tired of riding our bikes up and down the dead-end street our mother teaches us to pronounce with the harsh *ch*, as in "charge." *Char-jean.* As an adult, I wonder about its greater loveliness, had we borrowed it, like a loan word, from the French. As a child, I had wished to live in the adjacent neighborhood of Ramblewood with its endless possibilities of intersections, sprawling lots, and enviably big houses. How long has it been my habit to want to be elsewhere?

On the day of our family's visit, I notice, from the sidewalk, the campus parking sticker on the bumper of both cars parked in the neighbor's carport. Didn't the Lyndons also work at the college? I ask my mom. We knock, and Becky answers. I recognize her immediately.

"This is going to sound strange," I start, apologetic for the intrusion we were making before morning's fair start. "But I'm Jen Michel—well, Jen *Pollock* Michel—and our family used to live next door. You may remember my mom, Jan."

Becky gasps with the pleasantness of the surprise. "Jan! Jennifer! Why, of course!" Standing with the door propped open, she looks behind her toward the sinkful of breakfast dishes and smooths her hair.

"Come inside! Oh my goodness!" The Lyndons' house is a replica of our ranch, and we seat ourselves at a tiny table in the corner of the kitchen where our phone had also hung from the wall. I remember answering it on the day of my paternal grandfather's death. But despite the familiarity of the room, my mother is blank-faced.

"You don't remember me, Jan?" Becky asks, coloring. "We kept in touch until Mike died. I sent you a card when you married Don. You don't remember?" I want to tell Becky about my mother's breast cancer, the ravage of chemotherapy. These are reasons I could offer for her forgetting, but they are not reasons I believe.

My mother hesitates. "I don't know," she says slowly. "I can't remember that far back."

On our trip "home," I shake her loose for the perished things, like change from deep pockets. And hope for a sound.

I have lived the losing of home, intimately understanding how death has been from the very beginning humanity's greatest displacement. As Nicholas Wolterstorff discovered when his twenty-five-year-old son Eric died in a mountain-climbing accident, death is the sword of Damocles that hangs over home. When it falls, nothing remains the same, and in the wake of death, absence is the greatest qualifier of life. "I've become an alien in the world," Wolterstorff writes in his grief, "shyly touching it as if it's not mine. I don't belong any more. When someone loved leaves home, home becomes mere house."[3] Before the death of his son, Wolterstorff, a devout Christian philosopher, had tangoed with death intellectually, even offering theodicies in the

face of its menace. But after Eric died, death left him with a host
of unanswered questions—if also with continued hope. "I do not
know why God would watch him fall. I do not know why God
would watch me wounded. I cannot even guess. . . . Death is left
for God's overcoming."[4]

The sword falls on home—and some Son of God must bear it.

THE GOD OF THE WIDOW

In two pictures of divine judgment, sinners suffering the fateful
consequences of their rebellion are pictured as widows, struck
by sudden calamity. "How lonely sits the city," the prophet Jeremiah's lament begins. Jerusalem has been besieged and invaded
by the Babylonians because of its refusal to obey God. It smolders
in ruins. "How like a widow she has become, she who was great,"
Jeremiah cries (Lam 1:1). In the book of Revelation, Babylon,
allusive to all rebellious people, is destroyed, despite its self-
assured safety. "I sit as a queen," Babylon brags.

"I am no widow,
    and mourning I shall never see."
For this reason her plagues will come in a single day,
    death and mourning and famine. (Rev 18:7-8)

Babylon, ever the fool, has considered herself invulnerable to
destruction and asserted her power and prerogative as the guarantee of protection. But Babylon is struck down, suddenly ter-
rorized by the fragility of having been fated to be human. Death.
Without warning. Sudden and sure. The sword falls, and Babylon
is widowed.

Widows, in the Scripture, are classed among the most vulnerable people. When a husband died, with him died financial
security, political voice, and personal safety. Widows, along with
the fatherless and the immigrant, enjoyed no legal rights. As Job

decried, in ancient culture widows were at the hands of the merciless, who would enrich themselves by preying on their poverty, extending credit while simultaneously stealing the last security they enjoyed, taking a plowing animal, necessary for harvest, as pledge on the loan (Job 24:3). As defense of his righteousness Job cited his generosity toward the poor, which of course included the widow (Job 31:16-22). When the sword fell, it struck her first. She must be protected.

The widows were the needy of the Old Testament, and even though Job's story preceded the detailed provision for widow care as outlined in the Mosaic law, he understood the divine imperative to care for the defenseless. Widows in ancient cultures could not depend on government subsidies to pay the rent, buy food, and dress themselves for winter. Instead, they depended on the God who had promised to be a husband and on the community of his people, who were charged with their care. "Father of the fatherless and protector of widows is God in his holy habitation" (Ps 68:5). God is the God of the widow: he is her home, and to serve her is to serve him. As the apostle James insists in the New Testament, one sure sign of "religion that is pure and undefiled" is active care for the widow (Jas 1:27).

God made it a pressing obligation in the divine contract he tendered with Israel that they assume financial provision and legal protection for the widow. In a seven-year agricultural cycle, the tithes of the yields from the third and sixth years were set aside for the needy (Deut 14:28-29). At those harvest feasts, widows were hosted by the bounty of God's fields (plowed by another) and God's animals (raised by another). They received tangible expressions of God's goodness from the hand of their neighbor. In the final year of the cycle God forbade cultivation of the land: let the fields lay fallow, he commanded, "that the poor of your people may eat" (Ex 23:11). And he also forbade meticulous farming, which might look like numerous careful passes over a barley field or an olive orchard or a vineyard in the effort to prevent waste. Don't pick up anything that has been dropped or missed, God insists. "It shall be for the sojourner, the fatherless, and the widow" (Deut 24:19).

If God makes financial provision for widows, he also insures their legal protection. In ancient times land was transferred from father to son, and on exceptional occasions, when a family had no son, to a daughter. If there were no children to inherit a father's land, a brother, male cousin, or uncle would assume possession according to their kinsman-redeemer responsibilities (Num 27:1-11). These laws, of course, made no provision for the widow. But God declares that he is a God who "maintains the widow's boundaries" (Prov 15:25), and while there may be no formal provision for land transfer to a widow, the divine intent is to insure her safety and security. Perhaps the best example of God's benevolence to the widow are the laws governing levirate marriage, which command the brother of a dead husband to marry his widow and perform to her (and to his brother) his fraternal "duty" (Deut 25:5-10). He should hope to produce, by her, a son for his dead brother so "that his name may not be blotted out of Israel" (v. 6).[5] A son inherits the wife (or widow's) land and ensures the preservation of the inheritance as well as the family name. A son also protects his mother.

For as much careful attention as is given to the widow in the law, throughout Scripture she is often a faceless, nameless sufferer. Of the many important widow narratives in the Bible (the widow who feeds Elijah, the widow whose oil multiplies, the widow who gives her offering, the widow of Nain), it is striking that so few are named. Often their humanity, by omission of their names, seems stricken from the record. But perhaps the authorial neglect suggests how desperately invisible widows were in ancient culture. As Carolyn Custis James explains in her book *The Gospel of Ruth*, "The Hebrew word for widow (*almanah*) cemented a widow's low rank in ancient patriarchal culture. It comes from the root word *alem*, which means 'unable to speak.' In ancient patriarchal society, the widow was the 'silent one.'"[6]

Though the names of widows are eclipsed in many biblical stories, we need look no further than the genealogy of Jesus Christ to remember God's love for a widowed humanity and his claim on the perished things. In the first chapter of Matthew's Gospel the names of four women are included, and with certainty we can say that three were widowed: Tamar, daughter-in-law of Judah, who had carelessly forgotten his promise to her, leaving her stranded after the death of his son in the seclusion of her father's house; Ruth, the Moabite woman, who returns with her mother-in-law after the calamitous deaths of all the male members of Naomi's family; and "the wife of Uriah," who David had taken as his own and whose rightful husband he had murdered. Only Rahab, the prostitute, brothel host to Israelite spies, has uncertain marital status—though it is no stretch of the imagination to consider why a woman in ancient culture might undertake the scandal (and heartbreak) of such employment. Had she no man to protect and provide?

Tamar, Rahab, Ruth, Bathsheba: these are the women deserving mention in the genealogy of a king. Widows are not so invisible, God not so forgetful as we think. The gospel is hope for the perished things and home for all who grieve.

RUTH, THE MOABITE

One of these women, of course, steals the stage in an Old Testament book. She is an unlikely protagonist in the divine history, not least because she is a widow, but also because she is a Moabite, which is a tribe of people God has emphatically cursed. At the end of Ruth 1, Ruth has loyally returned to Israel on the arm of her mother-in-law, crossing the border and taking a sort of citizenship vow: "Your people shall be my people, and your God my God" (Ruth 1:16). She leaves her country and her people, promising stability in a new land with a new family. She will die here. If this is heroism, it will initially seem small and naive, for hers is a feral landscape. Widows and barren women are as useless as scorched, razed fields. How much help will Ruth contribute to fending off the vulnerability widows inevitably suffer, especially when her bodily safety cannot be guaranteed? And with her womb as dry as a gourd, what hope does she have at finding the "rest" of marriage to which Naomi so often refers? No reasonable man will marry her when she cannot bear him children.

This is the very human (and limited) perspective of the initial setting of the story. But it is Naomi's perspective, for she concludes that she "went away full [into Moab], and the LORD has brought me back empty" (Ruth 1:21). Reality, if that is what we want to call it, has embittered her. Widowhood is a vinegary gall, and she is unable to see beyond the distress of the everyday and the despair of the future. But the author of the book of Ruth doesn't allow us to entertain seriously Naomi's recounting of events. It is not so hopeless as it seems: for what Naomi calls fullness, at the beginning of the book, is really famine. (The family had initially left Israel in search of food.) And what she calls emptiness at the end of chapter one is really feast: "And they came to Bethlehem at the beginning of the barley harvest" (v. 22). Early it is intimated that the narrative is headed somewhere good and safe, even in the midst of the perished things.

The story of Ruth is no less the tale of one woman's risk and resourcefulness in the wake of tragedy. Ruth leaves her family of origin and the familiarity of home for a strange place and people when it would have been a safer alternative to choose as Orpah did—to stay. Yet she left, despite having so little to contribute to the cause of redemption. What she did offer, however, was moxie, which we see in Ruth 2:7: "Please let me glean and gather among the sheaves after the reapers," she has asked the field foremen, flouting what would have been traditional practice. As Custis James explains,

> Hired men went first—grasping handfuls of standing grain stalks with one hand, cutting them off at the base with a sickle, then laying the cut stalks on the ground. Female workers followed, gathering and binding cut grain into bundles to be carted to the threshing floor where raw kernels of grain were separated from the husks. Gleaners came last and were permitted in the field only *after* both teams of hired workers finished and bundled sheaves of grain were removed from the field.[7]

Ruth wasn't content with the back of the line. She asked for the pole position in the harvest train.

And this isn't Ruth's only brazen act. When Naomi suggests in chapter 4 that she show up at night at the threshing floor, after Boaz has feasted and imbibed, she is thinking only of the potential for marriage between the two. But when Ruth obeys her mother-in-law, laying down beside Boaz and "uncovering" the feet of the man who has shown her strange kindnesses, she dares to propose more. "I am Ruth, your servant," she says. "Spread your wings over your servant, for you are a redeemer" (Ruth 3:9). "In a single sentence she appeals to both the levirate and the kinsman-redeemer laws," writes Custis James.[8] She is asking not just for marriage but for the protection of the family land. "Ruth makes clear that her intention is to bear a child to inherit the land she is asking Boaz to redeem."[9] Against the odds Ruth is proposing marriage and entertaining motherhood. She is imagining, by faith, the possibilities for her life and for Naomi's. Rest. Home. Safety. Security. Something of greater permanence in this provisional life.

"May your house be like the house of Perez, whom Tamar bore to Judah," the village cheers as the story concludes (Ruth 4:12). They cite another woman, Tamar, known for her risk and resourcefulness, a woman who knew something of the perished things, something about vulnerability, something even about the failure of men to act in the moments of their great peril. Boaz and Ruth will marry; he has, at potentially great personal cost, agreed to acquire Elimelech's parcel of land and with it "Ruth, the Moabite, the widow of the dead" (Ruth 4:5). Boaz is a hero on two counts: first, he will perpetuate the name of the dead, rescuing Elimelech and Mahlon and Chilion from the strangling, suffocating, silencing power of death. But he will also rescue the widow, a sacrifice that catalyzes a chain reversal of fortunes. Ironically, the name of the nearest of Elimelech kin, who had refused the role of kinsman-redeemer ("I cannot redeem [the field] for myself, lest I impair my own inheritance" [Ruth 4:6]) is forgotten (and the widow remembered). A closed womb opens. And Naomi, bitter and barren, wrung out by the peril of perished things, nurses children. Calamity becomes conception because God is the God of the widow, and the shelter of his wings is sufficient shade. He will make a home for everyone who has survived the perished things.

I imagine Naomi singing in chorus with Sarah, whose God also made her laugh.

Who would have uttered to Abraham—
"Sarah is suckling sons!"[10]

Centuries later, an angel visits a young woman, and she takes fright at his words. A son? "How will this be, since I am a virgin?"

(Lk 1:35). A son of Ruth, Jesus Christ, is born and suckled at the breast of a young peasant girl. On him are cast the permanent hopes of humanity. "And he will reign over the house of Jacob forever, and of his kingdom there will be no end" (Lk 1:33). In Jesus' death, death is destroyed; in his resurrection, the perished things perish.

> Once for all I have sworn by my holiness;
>> I will not lie to David.
> His offspring shall endure forever,
>> his throne as long as the sun before me. (Ps 89:35-36)

Peace and permanence, good will to men.

151 GLENDON AVENUE
TORONTO, ONTARIO

I WILL LOSE HIM. I remember this on the night his blood sugar plummets and he lies limply on the bed. I kneel over him and the possibility of the perished things in a daze of helplessness. Years earlier, my husband, Ryan, a healthy thirty-year-old, had been diagnosed with Type I diabetes. But because I had been consumed with the care of our babies, I lent him little worry or fear. Ten years later, however, on the night he nearly falls unconscious before reaching clumsily for the bottle of sugar pills on the bedside table, I remember that marriage has not insulated me from fear but handcuffed me to it. I am more vulnerable than I have ever been, this two made one.

"Who will push me in my wheelchair when I'm older?" Ryan has asked our kids, teasing them about the possibility of his future decrepitude. On this night, I know with different certainty that he fears not aging but the slow creep of his disease. He fears losing his feet. Having lost his own father at forty-two, he fears widowing me young. So he writes me a letter in advance of his death, and I find it on his computer. "I love you," he assures before giving me the passwords to the bank accounts.

There is a mathematical sense that Ryan tries making of the world, and on this nearly comatose night, I understand better his desire to forecast predictions and simulate control, a rational impulse I have often regretted. "Every day, I am thinking of my diabetes," he tells me after our bed sheets soak with his sweat and he regains coherence. His words inspire new sympathy. And also fear.

Death will part us.

But of course I know this. Because I have lived this: the premature deaths of my father and brother were an early lesson in life's provisional nature. There is no controlling what we keep or for how long, and an earthly home is no measure of stability and safety, not really—not when lurking in the background of every day is the possibility that the phone will ring and life will lurch toward death. This is the brazenness of perished things. Mortality intrudes. Invulnerability dies. And at the end of it all, who will be there to have and to hold?

In this life there is no plugging up the holes of the unexpected worst, and every happy family is under threat of extinction. Perhaps this is what the apostle Paul means when he calls our bodies "tents" whose stakes can be pulled up without warning. "In this tent we groan, longing to put on our heavenly dwelling," he writes (2 Cor 5:2). We groan for permanence. We want to leave behind our mortal bodies and inhabit the "building from God, a house not made with hands, eternal in the heavens" (2 Cor 5:1). We long for the day when all things provisional, like every one of humanity's enemies, will be vanquished and put under the feet of a crucified, resurrected Jesus.

When the perishable [body] puts on the imperishable [body], and the mortal puts on immortality, then shall come to pass the saying that is written:

"Death is swallowed up in victory."
"O Death, where is your victory?
  O Death, where is your sting?" (1 Cor 15:54-55)

Death's death is the only hope for home.

The gospel, if it is to be good news, must denounce and decry the perished things in order for the world, once comprehensible and whole, to be put to rights, in order for us to regain an invulnerable, eternal, forever home. The only hope that can be called hopeful is Peter's living hope (1 Pet 1:3).

But here is reason to keep hope: the God-Man left his house, eternal in the heavens, and clothed himself with all of the liabilities of mortal, human flesh. He pitched his "tent" among us. In an act of great condescension and care, the I Am Who I Am, the Eternal God, endured the cold contingency of death for the sake of sinners. He did not rescue us with perishable things like silver and gold, but with the imperishable, precious blood of his own body. They call him the Man of Sorrows, and his sufferings have become his sympathies.

It shall be my theme in glory.

The best news of home is that Jesus did not stay dead. On the third day, he rose again. And bursting from the grave he reversed the unholy curse of impermanence. He put death under his feet. Sarah suckled sons. Naomi suckled sons. And the Son of God suckles us with forever hope—that a way has been made beyond the perished things, and we make it home.

Part II

THE WORK OF HOME

A SUFFERING SERVANT
The Labor of Love

ONE SLICE OF BREAD AND ONE PIECE OF BACON," our youngest daughter, Camille, explains dramatically, recalling the day she opened her lunch box to a destitute version of lunch.

"*One* slice of bread and *one* piece of bacon," she repeats for full effect, scanning the faces around the table for a reaction commensurate to the crime. David and Grace, a newly engaged couple, spectate the scene with bemusement. They've spent enough time with our family to know our dread of packing lunch boxes. They've heard us regularly hallow the monthly occasion of school-sponsored pizza lunch.

"I gave you grape tomatoes!" I defend, chagrined to remember we had run out of the lettuce and beefsteak tomatoes for the BLTs I had planned. True, I may have forgotten the mayonnaise. But hadn't I included, as redemptive gesture, a bag of chips? A cookie?

The prosecution rests her case.

I picture Camille at the lunch table, kids packed shoulder-to-shoulder as tightly as sardines, predatorily eyeing the contents of their neighbor's lunch box. One piece of bread, one slice of bacon, and a lidded bowl of grape tomatoes?

No one is taking care of me!

DOMESTIC MALAISE

What failed Camille was the housekeeping. Stephen Marche, writer and former editor of *Esquire*, takes up the housekeeping in his article for the *New York Times*, "The Case for Filth," both to cite its decline, if also to concede its importance. He notes that while women have reentered the work force in the latter half of the twentieth century, invariably consecrating less time to the care and keeping of their homes, their domestic partners have not picked up the slack. As research suggests, neither men nor women are ambitious to luster their furniture, much less to regularly dust. Marche proposes one workable solution to our modern domestic malaise: disinvestment. We should abandon the housekeeping. "Caring less is the hope of the future. House-work is perhaps the only political problem in which doing less and not caring are the solution, where apathy is the most progressive and sensible attitude," he writes.[1]

Nevertheless, despite his complaints about the work he calls "intimate drudgery," Marche grants a stubborn value inherent to the housework, which can't be estimated by numbering stacks of clean dishes, baskets of folded laundry, and (adequately packed) lunch boxes. In other words, housekeeping represents an intangible, emotional investment. As Marche underscores, the housekeeping is the "vaguer business of caring." Marche writes, "We all know families that are held together because [someone] knows who likes what in their sandwiches, who can or cannot read on a road trip, who needs cuddles after a hard day at school. The million tendernesses of 'emotional work' all require effort, often thankless effort."[2] I might despise washing thermoses and the assembly line motion of making sandwiches, but it is a logical impossibility to love my children and refuse to provide them lunch. To love is to labor. This is as true in our families as it is in the world, which God so loved. If God did not simply think benevolent thoughts on our behalf, if his welcome wrought work, should we take surprise at the unyielding obligations of love's housekeeping?

A life without the "intimate drudgery" of daily chores has long been cherished as the good life. Such is the utopian vision of Edward Bellamy's novel *Looking Backward*, published in the late 1880s. Protagonist Julian West, born in 1857, wakes up in the year 2000 and discovers a world in which industrial armies, rather than fathers and mothers, tend to the housekeeping. Public laundries and public kitchens do the dirty work from which individual homes are now exempt. In Bellamy's formulation, people are free to live the full and meaningful lives on which the housekeeping rudely intrudes.

Bellamy's novel was written at the moment in American history where "the servant problem" was the most discussed issue in the pages of women's magazines. As Glenna Matthews describes in her book *Just a Housewife*, in the late 1800s immigrants coming from Ireland and other parts of Europe began to replace American farm girls as domestics in urban households. But these "outsiders" were not familiar with American standards, and their poor job performance produced a swell of public complaint. Soon enough, however, servants were replaced by machines. By the 1920s the average American home was industrialized.[3] But Americans weren't merely buying gadgets for their home, for in with the vacuum swept the jubilant anticipation of freedom from keeping house. They were buying the good life, which is to say comfort apart from creatureliness. And isn't one of the enviable promises of material prosperity that we can buy an escape from household drudgery and eliminate the necessity of menial labor?

As Witold Rybczynski explains in *Home,* the goal of domestic technological innovation in the early twentieth century was less about economizing time and more about sparing physical labor. Most of the new appliances of the late nineteenth and early twentieth centuries were not, in fact, new. In the nineteenth century, women manually operated sewing machines, apple corers, eggbeaters, clothes washers, and dishwashers. But in the early twentieth century, when the home electrified, women began to be exempted from the onerous burden of housework so heavy upon their backs. They could begin keeping house in heels and pearls, or, as the feminists would have it, batik.

As media theorist Marshall McLuhan has explained in another context, technology has always acted like a prosthetic—a way to remove the body from the labor equation.[4] In this way household appliances were meant for delivering us from the age-old curse of "toil," which humans have suffered from since Genesis 3. These technological solutions in the home were not simply aimed at household convenience: they were a proposed means of salvation. One could be saved from the body as well as the burdens of the housekeeping.

A PRACTICE OF CREATURELINESS

In her short book *The Quotidian Mysteries,* Kathleen Norris explores the parallels between the routines of our domestic lives and the rhythms of our spiritual practice, begging us to see the importance of each. According to Norris, both are forms of the housekeeping. They depend on daily efforts and ordinary gestures; neither is once and done. Each requires a kind of liturgy, or routine, as an anchoring weight against the hosts of disordered desires that greet us in the morning before we've put a foot to the floor: selfish ambition, acedia, megalomania, greed. The liturgies of housework and practices like daily prayer ground us in a proper estimation of ourselves—we are creatures, not the Creator. Our quotidian routines return us to our bodies of dust, forging humility on the anvil of repetitive motion. We can't abandon the housekeeping, either the laundry or the liturgy, because it is one constraining element for human flourishing.

As Norris identifies, an early sign of mental distress is the neglect of the "daily personal and household chores," a telling indifference, which early monastics understood as the sin of acedia, or "lack of care." Like Esther, protagonist of Sylvia Plath's *The Bell Jar*, acedia is the unwillingness to do what must be redone: "The reason I hadn't washed my clothes or my hair was because it seemed so silly. . . . It seemed so silly to wash one day when I would have to wash again the next. It made me tired just to think of it. I wanted to do everything at once and for all and be through with it."[5] Acedia despises every Sisyphean gesture; it cannot be bothered by the housekeeping. We must beware the seduction of the easy-street life.

We need to recover the goodness of the housekeeping—and not simply because the findings of a recent survey report that 40 percent of millennials are no longer eating breakfast cereal because they "had to clean up after eating it."[6] We might survive weeks with unwashed socks, months with crumbs in our kitchen drawers, but we cannot sustain a lifetime without the care inextricably bound up in the housekeeping. And housekeeping, in the broad sense I am using it in the second half of this book, is not only meant to describe a narrow list of household chores. Instead, it is, as writes Marilynne Robinson in her essay "When I Was a Child," "a regime of small kindnesses, which taken together, make the world salubrious, savory, and warm. I think of [these] acts of comfort . . . as precisely sacramental."[7] Housekeeping points toward the thin places of daily life: where work, however monotonous and menial, becomes worship, witnessing to God's kingdom coming and his will being done, on earth as it is in heaven. In this sense, the effort to pour cereal and rinse clean one's bowl (even the bowl of one's neighbor) can be a spiritual practice, preparing us for greater exertion, more heroic love.

In the Hebrew Scriptures, the word *'avodah* shares the sense of "housekeeping" as I mean to use it, and it is translated in a variety of ways: work, service, labor, duties, ceremony, ministry. *'Avodah* is the word used to describe Jacob's fourteen years of laboring for Laban's daughter Rachel, as well as Israel's forced labor under repressive Egyptian taskmasters. It is also the word that signifies the priestly work of the tabernacle and temple. *'Avodah* reminds us that worship—and its attendant calls to vocation—can share the banality and ordinariness of everyday work.

Housekeeping, as worship and work, rightly relates us to God as well as to our fellow humans. In his book *Playing God*, Andy Crouch reminds readers that the Ten Commandments begin with the name of God and end with the word *neighbor*, providing an inherent address of the greatest temptations of our misuse of power: idolatry and injustice. "The lie that pulses at the heart of every act of idolatry and injustice," writes Crouch, "is that we are unfairly constrained by our promises, duties and obligations—all of which are marks of our creatureliness, our dependence and contingency on others—rather than graciously freed by them."[8] It's interesting to note that the first of the disciplines

Crouch suggests as a means for taming power is doing the dishes. Crouch, a busy author and speaker, frequently travels for work, leaving behind his wife and children and the banality of the housekeeping. He recognizes the tantalizing, devilish exchange he could make every time he boards a plane. He could trade dishes for crowds—*and be like God*. Instead, he does the dishes in advance of leaving, as just one small but important way to shape his relationship to his own power. "Dirty dishes remind me of my own creatureliness, my implication in and membership in the world's glorious mess."[9] Crouch stands at the sink, small and human, taking up the housekeeping as one way of taking up his proper place in the world.

Doing the dishes is a private practice with very public effects.

BENEFITS AND BURDENS

Housekeeping is one way to talk about the *burdens* of home and not just the *benefits*. We deceive ourselves in wishing to be freed to enjoy our blessings apart from the banality of our obligations; this is, in fact, one of the oldest of our greedy self-delusions. If we learn anything from the story of Eve and Adam's fall from grace, it might be the cheating impulse of desire. It is sin to reach for fruit without consideration of cost. And housekeeping is about cost—the cost of following a homemaking God, who bids us to make a home for others in this world. Housekeeping is a word representative of the church's vocation. As ones who know the Homemaker and his promise of home, we take up embodied, emplaced work as God's people: in our families and churches, our cities and neighborhoods. We labor for the sake of love.

The good news of the gospel reflects the inevitable logic between home and the housekeeping: humanity's benefits have been borne as burdens on the back of God. To be sure, our desire for home functions as a reliable signpost to the gift God intends to give to his people. It is, as C. S. Lewis most aptly said, the rainbow leading to the true pot of gold.[10] But this home, which God has made for his people, has always cost God the work of his housekeeping; his love has required his labor.

Housekeeping suitably describes the order and regularity to God's domestic method in Genesis 1–2, where it could seem as if God were taking his cues from a traditional housekeeping manual, which insists on the progression from higher to lower, dry to wet, inside to outside. Light and darkness are created first; sun and moon follow. Sky and earth and seas take shape; fowl, creeping things, and fish then inhabit the newly created spaces. If there is elbow in the effort, there is also logic in the approach. Importantly, all this ex nihilo energy is described as work that God rests from.

But creation may not be the clearest example of God's willingness to take up the housekeeping—to embrace, as Simone de Beauvoir has put it, the vice of immanence. In her 1949 book *The Second Sex*, which rose with the swelling tide of second-wave feminism, Simone de Beauvoir decried housework as the key impediment to women's liberation. "Woman is doomed to the continuation of the species and the care of the home—that is to say, immanence." In her estimation, "The healthy young woman will hardly be attracted by so gloomy a vice."[11] According to de Beauvoir, housekeeping represented not just banality but the oppression inherent to female domestic roles. The case for filth was a case for freedom.

But where God might have remained distant and removed from the mess we'd made of the world, he freely chose to enter it. The incarnation of God is the highest, holiest act of the housekeeping. God clothed his transcendent being with human flesh and condescended to earth. Interestingly, immanence shares a Latin root with the word *mansion*. To be immanent is to remain or dwell rather than transcend or rise above. Unlike Bellamy's utopian vision, God did not appoint an industrial army for the work of salvation. Contrary to our modern impulse for machinery, he chose no technological means to communicate his love. Instead, he dwelled among us. In a body. Taking up the bloody, "vague" business of caring.

Home, as I hope we will see in the second half of this book, is not only reward. It is also responsibility. Our good Father is calling us home, though not just for the sake of ourselves. Henri Nouwen began to understand the dual dimensions of home—love and labor, blessing and burden, reward and responsibility—as he studied Rembrandt's painting *Prodigal Son* and meditated on the famous Gospel parable. The painting and parable put him in touch with his "yearning for a final return, an unambiguous sense of safety, a lasting home."[12] But as Nouwen began to see his own sins of alienation and consider that Jesus became the prodigal Son for us, his exploration did not end there. Soon Nouwen came to see the responsibilities inherent to receiving God's love. "Do I want to be not just the one who is being forgiven, but also the one who forgives; not just the one who is being welcomed home, but also the one who welcomes home; not just the one who receives compassion, but the one who offers it as well?"[13] Nouwen saw that the parable was not content to leave him a son, dining at the feast, but endeavored to position him as father, preparing the table.

Nouwen discovered the benediction of home—that if it blesses, it also sends.

JOSEPH, A SERVANT IN EGYPT

Joseph is an ancient example of a man who kept house. After he is sold by his brothers into slavery, he is elevated to the role of steward in three separate houses: first, the house of Potiphar;

then, the Egyptian prison house; and finally, the house of Pharaoh. As Robert Alter notes in his commentary, five words are consistently repeated throughout these texts: *all, hand, house, blessing, succeed.*[14] *Hand*, as a word that recalls embodiment, and *house*, as a word that recalls emplacement, both illuminate the nature of Joseph's holy housekeeping.

When Joseph is bought "from the *hands* of the Ishmaelites" and becomes Potiphar's slave, he quickly gains his master's favor and rises in household rank, eventually to be named "overseer of the house" (Gen 39:1, 4, Alter's translation). What's immediately clear is that *house* is broad in intent, for Joseph has oversight over everything Potiphar owns, with two exceptions: the food on his table and his wife. Joseph superintends the affairs of the household. He sees to the business of the fields. So capable is his domestic management and so evident the Lord's blessing on his housekeeping that Potiphar "left all that he had in Joseph's *hands*" (v. 6, Alter's translation). Most interestingly, the textual evidence points to Joseph's housekeeping work as priestly work, a dimension obscured by translations like the ESV but highlighted in Alter's translation. This same Hebrew word, *sharath*, is the precise word used to describe Aaron's work at the altar of God. Joseph is keeping house for Potiphar just as the priests kept house for God, modeling for us what it means to work in the world "as for the Lord" (Col 3:23). Every desk, every kitchen sink, every hospital room, and every field acts as an altar where we present our work—even the housekeeping—as worship.

As readers familiar with the story will remember, Joseph is falsely accused of rape by Potiphar's wife and is immediately thrown into prison. But this isn't just a prison: it's a prison *house.*[15] This second episode of Joseph's life in Egypt reprises many of the same elements from the previous episode. God grants Joseph favor; he rises in rank among the other prisoners.

The "master of the house"—the prison warden—begins entrusting authority and responsibility into the "hands" of Joseph. Joseph becomes a steward, managing on behalf of the warden the affairs of the prison and its prisoners, and again the Hebrew describes Joseph's service as ministry: "He ministered to [the chief cupbearer and chief baker]" (Gen 40:4, Alter's translation). Joseph, emplaced in a *house*, works with his *hands*—and his ministry of housekeeping (in this case, the care and keeping of two celebrity prisoners) eventually delivers him into another house two years later, where he is later remembered for his ability to interpret dreams.

At the suggestion of the chief cupbearer, Joseph is called to Pharaoh's side to interpret his troubling dreams, and as the story goes, when he does he is suddenly promoted to the highest rank in the kingdom after Pharaoh himself. What should now no longer be a surprise to us as readers is the author's insistence on the kingdom as a *house:* "After God has made known to you all this, there is none as discerning and wise as you. You shall be over my *house*" (Gen 41:40, Alter's translation). As a symbol of Joseph's newly invested authority to take up the housekeeping for the kingdom of Egypt, preparing stores of grain in the seven years of plenty for the seven years of famine, Pharaoh takes the ring from his *hand* and puts it on Joseph's *hand*.

Joseph's housekeeping, enabled by God, saves people from starvation. For Jacob's family, for Egypt, and for the entire region, housework—the administration of grain collection, storage, and distribution—is the means of salvation. God appointed no magical methods for staving off death: rescue was in this instance (and, as I would argue, in every) a work of the *hands*. As Alter notes in his commentary, when Genesis 41:47 mentions the "gatherings" made during the seven years of plenty, the Hebrew word is most precisely "handfuls."[16] Joseph kept house for God, and a people who suffered from famine were saved. Quite curiously, in relaying his story of housekeeping when he finally reveals his identity to his brothers, Joseph speaks in the terms that Nouwen has suggested in *The Return of the Prodigal Son*: "It is not you who sent me here but God, and He has made me *father* to Pharaoh and lord to all his house and ruler over all the land of Egypt" (Gen 45:8-9). The son and brother, stripped of home, became a father, providing a welcome for the very brothers who had intended to murder him. God purposed "sustenance" through Joseph's housekeeping. Through Joseph, he would "preserve life" (v. 7). Joseph's story illustrates that God gets his work done in the world by the willing hands of his people.

But there was yet to come a greater Joseph, who was not simply a servant in his Master's house, but a Son. He took up the housekeeping, saving his people from a worse fate than famine. As the Gospel writer John explained, he came to drink and pour a cup—the abundant, overflowing cup of life (Jn 10:10).

JESUS, THE SUFFERING SERVANT

In the second half of the book of Isaiah, the melody of four "Servant Songs" rises out of the silent ash of exile. While the first half of Isaiah portends the devastation of Babylonian conquest, the second half of Isaiah is postexilic in vision and hope. The second half of the book features the vision of a servant to be sent by God, a servant unlike faithless Israel, whose many sins of rebellion have been enumerated in the prophetic record.

"Behold my servant," the first song begins in Isaiah 42 (vv. 1-9). This servant is a man who has been handpicked by God, a man the Spirit of God dwells in, a man God takes unabashed delight in. And God has chosen him for a particular task: the advance of justice. Three times, justice sounds like a dinner gong in Isaiah 42. The servant's housekeeping will restore to the home the

justice it has lacked since the day when the door shut behind
Adam and Eve and murder crept into the first human family. The
weak will be defended. The fragile will be sheltered. God's
servant will help those most unable to help themselves: the blind,
the imprisoned, all those who sit in darkness. He will deal with
human rebellion, which has flagrantly flouted the Ten Words
and traded worship for idolatry, justice for injustice. But this
servant's housekeeping is not just restoring goodness to the home
but glory to the homemaker. As a faithful servant, he concerns
himself with his master's name rather than his own.

In the second servant song (Is 49:1-7), the servant descends
into human history as every woman and man must: from the
womb, "from the body of my mother." Thrust through the canal
of blood and water, he emerges in wriggling form, dressed like
a warrior. His mouth is like a "sharp sword," his body a "polished
arrow." Lit like a beacon, this servant is a "light for the nations,"
who God intends to bring back home by way of the moun-
tainous roads and the highways he will raise up. For the first time
the suffering of this servant is intimated: he will be "deeply despised, abhorred by the nation." But though he will suffer dis-
grace and become the servant of rulers, he will not always assume
such a lowly rank: his right and recompense rest with God. Isaiah
anticipates the day when every knee shall bow and every tongue
confess the name of this chosen servant, whose mission it is to
proclaim salvation to the end of the earth. This servant's "labor"
shall not be in vain.

In the third servant song (Is 50:4-9), the work of the servant
relieves the weariness of the world. He labors for their rest. His
life is not self-determined; rather, he demonstrates the holiness
of the listening life, waking each morning to the sound of his
master's voice.[17] The servant offers his body to the blows and
spittle of injustice; back, cheeks, face. But he does not flinch or

flee. Rather, he sets his face like flint toward Jerusalem, knowing the joy set before him when he has endured the housekeeping. "I shall not be put to shame" is this prophet's strange confidence amidst misfortune and mistreatment (v. 7).

The fourth and final servant song is the most familiar to our ears, and it sounds baleful notes of suffering. Though the melody has lifted in the previous chapter, announcing a tune of joy ("The voice of your watchmen—they lift up their voice; / together they sing for joy; / for eye to eye they see / the return of the LORD" [Is 52:8]), it is clear that a high price must be paid for that homecoming. If the Lord is to return, if the people are to return, if Jerusalem is to be redeemed—and home reinhabited—then a servant must suffer the debt of the housekeeping. For a city to flourish, a man must flail, becoming despised, rejected, stricken, smitten, afflicted, pierced, and crushed. "The LORD has laid on *the body of the servant* the iniquity of us all" (Is 53:6, my paraphrase). "Who would have thought God's saving power would look like this?" (Is 53:1 *The Message*). In the story of home as the gospel tells it, a servant suffers and dies at the hands of his master—because "it was the will of the LORD to crush him" (v. 10).

Jesus is the Suffering Servant, and the cross is the ultimate life-preserving act of cosmic housekeeping. Similar to Joseph's ministry in Potiphar's house, the prison house, and the house of Egypt, this servant's housekeeping—the act of offering his own body—is a priestly sacrifice. But unlike Old Testament animal sacrifices, which had to be repeated annually, the body that had been prepared for him was a final, perfect sacrifice (Heb 9:24-28) received by God for the sustenance of the world. "I am among you as the one who serves," Jesus said to his disciples (Lk 22:27). "I have given you an example, that you also should do just as I have done to you. Truly, truly, I say to you, a servant is not greater than his master, nor is a messenger greater than the one who sent him" (Jn 13:15-16). And if Jesus has taken up the housekeeping—the embodied, emplaced labor of love—we should never consider ourselves exempt.

In his book *The Jesus Way*, Eugene Peterson discusses these four servant songs, noting our disdain for the housekeeping. "Nobody aspires to be a servant. We have a higher opinion of ourselves."[18] Yet Peterson says we cannot avoid the call to servanthood in our life with God, for it is foundational to the way God was at work in Jesus and the way he continues his saving work through his church, a work of the *hands*. Peterson notes the two-dimensional direction of servanthood: it is both offered to God as well as offered to our neighbor—or, in his words, "The servant serves God by serving the sinner."[19] Though there is only one true Servant, Jesus Christ, though the "cross is unrepeatable," there are many servants following in his stead, and "cross-*bearing* is not."[20]

Housekeeping—acts of service to God for the sake of the sinner—is still required if everyone is to find his way home. And this is why our book turns here in a more practical direction. Like Joseph, like Jesus, we, the church, must be about our Master's business.

151 GLENDON AVENUE
TORONTO, ONTARIO

THE SNOW HAS FALLEN PREMATURELY in November, and on this bleak Monday morning, winter is an unexpected guest. After breakfast, in their rush to get ready for school, the children overturn the baskets in the mudroom, sorting through umbrellas and library books, sunglasses and sunscreen. They fish out hats and gloves before stepping into the season's new boots.

"I like this, Mom," our youngest son, Colin, says proudly, tracing the red outline along the sole of his new boot. "And I like that they're shiny," he adds, noting their near-iridescent blue. His twin brother, whose feet are one size smaller, looks dejectedly at his pair of hand-me-downs.

The six of us finally pile into the car, and as we back out of the driveway, the sky falls thick and white around us. "Look at the birds of the air, and consider the lilies of the field," Jesus had once preached to a gathered crowd seated on a mountainside. In the Sermon on the Mount he was reminding his listeners of the diligence of God's housekeeping and its credible testimony of God's care: the birds eat what they do not gather and store in barns; the lilies are elegantly dressed, having spent no vain worry about what to wear.

Creation is a testament to God's good housekeeping. "What is man that you are mindful of him, / and the son of man that you care for him?" (Ps 8:4). The psalmist has caught himself, on one particular evening, in a mood of holy marvel. The inky black sky is threaded with luminosity: with his eyes, he traces the outline of the Big Dipper. He finds his way to the Orion. This man, living long before Copernicus and the Hubble telescope, shares no knowledge that the earth revolves around the sun. He cannot know that our sun is one of 200 billion stars in our galaxy, our galaxy one of 100 billion galaxies in the universe. But with the naked eye he perceives glory in "the heavens, the work of your fingers, the moon and the stars, which you have set in place." Yet the psalmist is stunned, not simply by the sky's grandeur but by God's mindfulness toward humanity. In a world so vast and underneath a sky so brilliant, why does God preoccupy himself with mortals and their finitude? "O LORD, our Lord, how majestic is your name in all the earth!"

There is indeed a strange juxtaposition in Psalm 8. At first the psalmist declares the glory and majesty of God. But that initial awe is not followed by any lengthy exposition of God's holy remove from creation. There are no images to inspire human fear and trembling. Rather, the beauty of the constellations make the psalmist think not of God's transcendence but of his immanence. The stars, distant and out of reach, strangely commend God's nearness and care.

In Psalm 8 the great and glorious God is near and stooped low. In fact, for all that is magisterial about God, the royalty language in this psalm is mostly reserved for humanity: he, the "son of man" is "crowned with glory and honor"; he has "dominion" over creation; and as evidence of God's willingness to share glory and honor, even authority, he puts "all things under his feet." Of course the New Testament ascribes this psalm to Jesus Christ, who came as God clothed in human flesh (Heb 2). But God's bequeathed dignity is not reserved for Jesus alone, for Jesus partook of humanity in order that we could know something of the wild width, breadth, height, and depth of the divine love for us.

God's goodness is as bewildering and breathtaking as this psalm suggests to us, not least because, in contrast to the glory of the skies, we understand something of our smallness and in-dignity. There is much to suggest that we do not warrant divine attention. Nevertheless, as Matthew Henry writes in his commentary, "God's goodness *is* his glory."

We don't know to expect God's mindfulness toward us—but his housekeeping makes our hearts sing.

7

HOUSE OF GOD
The Church as Home

383 JARVIS
TORONTO, ONTARIO

My HAND GLIDES ALONG THE BANISTER as we climb the carpeted, creaky staircase and wind our way to the third floor. *Let us stay*, I pray. Grace Toronto Church, which calls itself a "church for the city in the city," has just recently purchased this historic stone church building at the corners of Jarvis and Carlton Streets, a neighborhood in which some of Toronto's most prominent families originally settled and which now hosts a diversity of residents—many making their homes on the park benches of Allan Gardens. Our church is putting down roots along this corridor of the city where rich and poor collide. After a series of building renovations, 383 Jarvis will be our permanent home.

This past fall Ryan and I served on a team of lay leaders for the church's capital campaign, pledging to give what might have been a partial down payment on a house in the city. But for whatever we might lose in terms of potential home ownership, we gain in greater stability. Like our pastor has said, "This building is going to outlast all of us." And he's right: people come and go, driven by the winds of mobility. Even a lifetime anchored down is perilously brief. But churches, especially those who intentionally choose to root themselves deeply in their places, have staying power. The church is the real host of home.

Numerous church congregations have worshiped at 383 Jarvis, and the building was most recently co-owned by St. Andrew's Estonian Evangelical Lutheran Church and St. Andrew's Lutheran Latvian Church. These two aging, shrinking congregations lived the losing of home during the Second World War when the Russian Army occupied Estonia and pushed tens of thousands of refugees into the sea; many thousands died in the treacherous crossing to Sweden. As the *National Post* reported in an interview with Eneri Taul, a member of the Estonian congregation, the country lost one quarter of its population during World War II. "When it was over, there was no going home. But there was Canada."[1]

Taul was bundled by her mother into a leaky fishing trawler with other Estonians fleeing the Russian fighter planes and submarines; she came to Canada when she was two. Her harrowing journey toward finding a new home is depicted in the large stained glass window purchased and installed by the congregation in the 1980s in the stone building of 383 Jarvis. "It faces south toward Lake Ontario. Toward the water, where so many refugee stories begin."[2] Like the stained glass windows of medieval European cathedrals, which told the biblical stories to an illiterate populace, these panes, etched with the stories of refugees, tell the painful stories of permanent goodbyes. And yet the real point of the refugee window is deeply theological: placed in a sanctuary, it reminds us that the church of Jesus Christ bids all of us welcome. The gospel is hope for all the wandering lost.

A HOUSE FOR GOD

Church buildings are not, of course, the church. The church is the people of God. As the apostle Peter explained, women and men, children and elderly, are the bricks and mortar of God's present-day temple (1 Pet 2:5). But while the church, elsewhere described as the body and bride of Christ, is not the building, this does not mean that the material aspect of church—its building and neighborhood—are immaterial matters.

Striking in the Old Testament accounts of tabernacle and temple worship are the material details of Israel's worship. In Exodus the people of God pitch a tent as a dwelling place for God; they call it the tabernacle. Like the patriarchs, the Israelites are afoot, headed toward the promises of God. Their wilderness journey out of Egypt into Canaan was intended to have been much briefer, but when the people rebel at Kadesh Barnea, God sentences them to forty years of wandering. Nevertheless, rather than having his people build altars at each way station in the desert, God commands Moses to lead a capital campaign, raising not money but precious metals, colorful yarns, fine linen, goats' hair, tanned rams' skins, goatskins, acacia wood, oil, spices, and precious gems. "Let them make me a sanctuary, that I may dwell in their midst," God commands (Ex 25:8)—the Hebrew word for sanctuary, *miqdash*, means "abode." In a strange reversal of Genesis 1–2, where God made a home for his people, now the people are instructed to make a home for God.

The book of Exodus is consumed with the Israelites' acts of sacred housekeeping: seven chapters are dedicated to the instructions given to Moses, the divine "pattern" given by God; six chapters are dedicated to the execution of the instructions and completion of the tabernacle. Details are not spared in terms of the furnishings for God's house (the ark, the table of the bread of the Presence, the golden lampstand, the bronze altar, the altar of incense) or the accessories required for the rituals of proper worship. As Robert Altar notes in his commentary, "Every one of the utensils required for the elaborate procedure of catching the blood of an animal, shoveling up the ashes and residual fat (*deshen*), turning over the meat as it burns, raking off the coals from the fire, is patiently catalogued in this non-narrative material."[3] There is yawning attention paid to the domestic details of the tabernacle in Exodus, and it tends to bore the biblical reader, who aches for real action. But as Alter notes,

> The satisfaction this material gives its audience is not story but pageantry: the splendor of the many-colored textiles displayed along the walls of the Tabernacle, the bronze loops on which they are hung, the wrought precious metals and inlaid gems of the various ritual implements. . . . Human labor, scrupulously following a divine plan, creates an ordered space that mirrors the harmony of God's creation.[4]

Exodus details the construction of the tabernacle not because it moves the plot of the story forward but because it is its own act of generous worship. No expense is spared for the housekeeping, which artisans, uniquely filled with the Spirit of God, are commissioned to assume (Ex 36:30-35). Entire industries are implicated in the domestic project: spinning, weaving, tanning, carpentry, metalworking, and embroidery. In fact, many of these industries are predominantly female, and as the text makes explicit, the women are notably enthused about contributing to the work. They donate their brooches and earrings, rings and pendants, purportedly elbowing ahead of the men in their worshipful eagerness.[5]

Women and men generously make a home for God, which although mobile is also beautiful. But the text does not make their housekeeping central to its purpose. As John Sailhamer writes in his commentary on Genesis, "The instructions for the work of building the tabernacle are written in such a way that they provide an interesting parallel to God's own work of creation recorded in Genesis 1."[6] Sailhamer offers these specific parallels between the creation narratives of Genesis and the tabernacle passages of Exodus: first, just as the creation is ordered in seven acts, each prefaced by the refrain, "And God said," the instruction for building the tabernacle is divided into seven acts also introduced by the phrase, "And the LORD said." Additionally, the Garden of Eden boasts gold and precious jewels and is protected by the cherubim; likewise, the tabernacle is constructed with precious metals and gems, and the ark is protected by the golden cherubim. Third, when God finished his work of creation, he inspected it and declared it good; when the tabernacle was completed, Moses also inspected the finished work and declared it good. Fourth, in the creation accounts humanity is made in the image of God; in the tabernacle accounts the tent is made according to the divine pattern. And finally, just as the creation narratives are followed by the fall, so the two tabernacle passages are interrupted by human folly: the worship of the golden calf. As a tent pitched for the God who once walked with our human parents in the garden, the tabernacle is a move toward restoring the fellowship that was lost as a result of Eve and Adam's rebellion.

The tabernacle pointed back toward creation as both home for humanity as well as home for God. This is the salient point of Old Testament scholar John H. Walton's book *The Lost World of Genesis One*, which avoids typical creation debates and focuses instead on ancient cosmology and the account of creation (according to that cosmology) as an ordered system of functions. As God sorts and separates, he gives function to the various elements of sky and earth, and these functions are meant for the benefit of humanity, who the cosmos is made for. "Throughout Genesis 1," Walton writes, "the refrain 'it was good' expressed the functional readiness of the cosmos for human beings."[7] Walton highlights the difference between the creation account according to Genesis and the creation accounts of other ancient cultures: "Whereas in the rest of the ancient world creation was set up to serve the gods, a theocentric view, in Genesis, creation is not set up for the benefit of God but for the benefit of humanity—an anthropocentric view. Thus we can say that humanity is the climax of the creation account."[8] In the beginning, God was the cosmic host, humanity his welcome guests.

But if the world God made is a home for his people, it was also a home for himself—or better yet, a temple. According to Walton, ancient readers would have immediately understood that Genesis 1, concluding with God's rest, was a temple text: "Deity rests in a temple, and only in a temple," notes Walton.[9] In the *Enuma Elish*, the Babylonian creation epic, after Marduk defeats his enemies and completes his creative acts, he is enthroned in his temple in the city of Babylon. In the Genesis account, after God breathes his life into Adam and Eve, he rests, inhabiting his temple. Walton notes that Psalm 132 brings together the themes of divine rest, temple, and enthronement:

> "Let us go to his dwelling place;
>   let us worship at his footstool!"
> Arise, O LORD, and come to your resting place,
> you and the art of your might. . . .
> For the LORD has chosen Zion,
>   he has desired it for his dwelling place:
> "This is my resting place for ever and ever;
>   here I will dwell, for I have desired it." (Ps 132:7-8, 13-14)

When God rests, he rests in his temple, and Genesis 2:1-3 pictures the Creator resting in his creation. In other words, humanity's home, built by God, is a temple—and God's tabernacle, built by humanity, is a home. The tabernacle was, of course, no permanent home for God; it was a provisional one inhabited by a God who so radically identified with his people as to sojourn with them. Israel was a wandering people, and in a strange sense, the God of Israel's tabernacle was a wandering God. For forty years his royal tent was pitched in the middle of their camp.

Centuries later David plans to build a more permanent house of God, although it is his son, Solomon, who completes the project. Solomon recognizes, however, that no house or temple can contain the limitlessness that is God. "Behold, heaven and the highest heaven cannot contain you, how much less this house that I have built!" Solomon confesses in his public prayer of dedication when the majestic temple, overlaid with gold, is complete (2 Chron 6:18). Solomon bears no illusions that an infinite God can inhabit a finite space in finite time, and yet he asks God to favor the sacred space for the good of Israel: to hear the nation's prayers, to forgive its sins, to heal its land. As the grand temple ceremony closes and Solomon bids God to take his rest, fire falls from heaven and consumes the sacrifices, and "the glory of the LORD filled the LORD's house" (2 Chron 7:2). Like all houses, God's house has its own smell: the "burning of incense of sweet spices," the smell of the "regular arrangement of the showbread," and the aroma of "the burnt offerings [sacrificed] morning and evening" (2 Chron 2:4). God's house, like a busy, bustling kitchen in the hours stretching before dinner, smells like welcome.

THE CHURCH AS HOME

In *The Confessions* Augustine tells the conversion story of Marius Victorinus, an honored philosopher in ancient Rome whose statue stood in the Roman forum. Before his baptism as a Christian he had vigorously defended the idolatrous Roman cults. After his study of the Scriptures, Victorinus was converted, though he did not immediately pursue membership in the Christian church. "He was afraid to offend his friends, proud devil-worshippers," Augustine concluded. Victorinus did, however, privately announce his conversion to Simplicianus, a church leader. "Did you know that I am already a Christian?" he asked eagerly. "I shall not believe that," said Simplicianus, "or count you among the Christians unless I see you in the Church of Christ."[10]

This is a strange story for evangelical ears. Today, we can hardly imagine refusing recognition of someone's sincere confession of faith or of making salvation conditional on church membership. Yet sixteen hundred years ago this was an agreed-upon formulation of obedient Christian faith: if a person wanted to follow Jesus, they joined the church.

Seismic shifts in thinking have occurred between Augustine's day and ours, not least of which is the emphasis on the individual rather than the collective. Today, we're tempted to privatize our faith. Church membership is presented as one of many appealing choices in the spiritual growth cafeteria line, participation in a local church as optional as pie. Spiritually, there's no real sense of *need* for church, only preference.

But according to the language of Scripture, we cannot divorce ourselves from the church any more easily than we could cut off our hand or renounce our blood lines. The church is the believers' new family. It is *home*. When Jesus was reminded by his disciples that his mother and brothers were anxious to speak to him and prevented by the crowds from reaching him, Jesus answered, "My mother and my brothers are those who hear the word of God and do it" (Lk 8:21). He did not define his family according to blood relationship but according to spiritual ties, demonstrating that a believer's primary relationships are not those of their biological family. Instead, the Christian pledges first allegiance to a new household of faith.

The domestic term *household* is the metaphor the apostle Paul uses to describe the church in his first letter to Timothy. In the church, where everyone is regarded as family, older men should be treated as fathers, younger men as brothers; older women regarded as mothers, younger women as sisters. While this doesn't exempt women and men from direct responsibilities to their families of origin and marriage, it does mean that everyone gets a family. As is clear in 1 Timothy 5, which details the principles governing the care for widows, when a widow has no relatives to look after her, the church will be to her a family.

In his book *Spiritual Friendship* Wesley Hill explores the reconfiguration of human relationships in light of the gospel, arguing for a return to promise-bound friendships sustained by the church. He notes the diminishing importance of friendship in contemporary culture and identifies several reasons for our disinterest in keeping at the housekeeping of Christian community, including our modern mythology of marriage. As the story goes today, the relationship of ultimate significance is the wedded love of husband and wife; second to it is the loyalty that parents have to their children. Unfortunately, however, this limited conception of "home"—as the shared space of the nuclear family—leaves a lot of people out, including Hill, a gay Christian pledged to celibacy. He cites the architectural shift in England from the great medieval hall, "which in former times had been the places for gentlemen to display their friendships through public gestures of affection," to small dining rooms—or marital spaces.[11] Retreat and isolation continues to be hardwired into much of our built environment—to the peril of home as God intended it.

The church, Hill argues, must bear witness to bonds of human love and loyalty that exist outside of the marriage covenant—to a home that exists outside of the nuclear family. "A great company of saints witnesses to the fact that we can indeed flourish without romance, marriage, or children; I don't know of one who witnesses to the possibility of our flourishing without love altogether."[12] Hill writes of looking for a place to put his love. A *home*, in other words.

WELCOME AND BELONGING

The church is *home*, and part of our daily housekeeping is learning to belong to one another. If this is good news for the unmarried, it is also good news for me. The nuclear family cannot bear the full weight of human hope and expectation, struggle and need. It's too fragile and human an entity. As a married woman with children, I need relational connection and commitment beyond the circle of my immediate family, both for myself as well as for the sake of my family.

According to the Scriptures, it is not parents alone who are responsible for the love and nurture of our children: the church participates in this task with us. This divinely ordained cooperation is recognized at every baby's dedication or baptism. At that holy moment when the pastor prays (and the infant cries), church and family together commit to partnership. James K. A. Smith writes that at a child's baptism (Smith is a paedobaptist) bloodlines are relativized, and the nuclear family rejects the modern domestic ideal of the family as "closed, self-sufficient autonomous unit."[13] Quoting Alexander Schmemann, Smith writes, "The promises in baptism indicate a very different theology of the family, which recognizes that 'families work well when we do not expect them to give us all we need.'"[14] But whether we baptize our infants or not, the principle is the same: our active participation in the church—and our willingness to see it as home—relieves some of the onerous burdens of childrearing, often made heaviest by our sense of limitation.

We can't parent alone. And we aren't meant to. We have friends—better, brothers and sisters, aunts and uncles—to help carry some of the worry and weight of the family housekeeping. And as I've learned from recent research, the most important predictor of whether children from Christian families keep their faith into adulthood is the number of multigenerational connections they enjoy at church. Teenagers may not need a youth group populated by hundreds of peers, but they do need other Christian adults in their church to take an interest in them and communicate that they belong.

I doubt my unmarried friends know my gratitude for their friendship—how they willingly abide the din of dribbling basketballs in the front hallway to linger over Saturday brunch and easily forgive long stretches of unintended silence when I fail to call. I imagine they see themselves in the role of taker rather than giver in the relationship, but I'd like to assure them that their presence in our home immediately changes the dynamic of our family, especially now that there are teenagers in the house, who are nearly catatonic with the boredom that is their parents. These friends bring with them a sense of play that parents, mired in the routine of daily family life, forget. Once, two women from our church spent hours designing and baking our house in gingerbread, then more hours decorating it with our children on a gloomy Saturday afternoon. Those were five wonderful hours of company keeping that I would not, in all my pragmatism, have ever thought to plan. But I'm grateful they did because it made our house feel more like home.

It is not easy to stretch across the demographic differences of our lives and make a go at community. But this is part of the church's housekeeping. If home is God's welcome, then each of us must work to make sure everyone belongs. God has a home, and he is looking to share it. As the psalmist describes him, he is "Father of the fatherless and protector of widows. . . . God settles the solitary in a home" (Ps 68:5-6).

FAITHFUL PRESENCE

Church becomes family for its members; it also can become home for its community. Paul Sparks, Tim Soerens, and Dwight Friesen, coauthors of *The New Parish* and cofounders of the Parish Collective, are trying to help churches become faithfully present in their local communities and take up their house-keeping obligations of justice and mercy. They recognize the temptation that we individually and churches corporately face to live "above" our places, remaining essentially disconnected from the desires and disappointments of our closest neighbors. They write, "We think there is a deep connection between Adam and Eve's calling to care for a specific place, and God's instruction not to eat from the tree of knowledge. After all, grasping Godlike knowledge at the expense of relationship is a way of attempting to transcend your boundaries. It is a way of avoiding both your limitations and your responsibilities."[15]

As C. Christopher Smith and John Pattison write in *Slow Church*, we cannot hurry the church's work of faithful presence, which is rooted in a particular place and committed to blessing a particular group of people. If Jesus has loved the world, the church must love its city. "We need practices," they write, "that will orient our desires to our places . . . [We should leave off] broad generalities about changing the world [and instead] re-imagine in more specific ways that transformation of our own particular places."[16] Having been made in the image of a home-making God, whose persistent concern is for our flourishing, the church must share his desire for the world's habitability—for both the spiritual and material concerns of its neighbors.

It is the work of the housekeeping that Grace Toronto Church remembers every week in its liturgy as we pray for the church and the city. We take up, for the content of this corporate prayer, the church bulletin as well as the local newspaper. (Inevitably, every time it is my turn to lead this part of the service, I cry, and my children greet me smirking after I've finished and have found my seat.) We pray for the church's ministries, and we pray for the city's police officers. We pray for our staff, and we pray for the Toronto District School board. We pray for upcoming church events, and we pray for the ongoing work of the Canadian federal government, which has just recently gladly welcomed, in a handful of weeks, twenty-five thousand Syrian refugees. And then, in expression of our willingness to be an answer to our prayers, we partner with city organizations to help children in crisis, homeless youth, and women facing unwanted pregnancy. Having interceded for justice, we endeavor to act justly.

It is not accidental that among the first evidences of conversion in Acts is renewed commitment to generosity and mission. Quite spontaneously, as men and women are baptized and begin to see their lives reoriented to a new kingdom and a greater King, people change their patterns of consumption. They begin sacrificing their financial resources for the good of their new brothers and sisters and the ongoing work of witness and worship. As Acts 2:44-46 explains, the new believers "were together and had all things in common. And they were selling their possessions and belongings and distributing the proceeds to all, as any had need. And day by day, attending the temple together and breaking bread in their homes, they received their food with *glad* and *generous* hearts" (emphasis added). Glad generosity is undeniable evidence that the gospel of Jesus Christ—the God who left home and made himself poor—is taking deep root in the human heart. The church is only the church when it pours itself out for the hungry and satisfies the desire of the afflicted (Is 58:10). Generosity makes a home for our cities' homeless.

In her book *Kingdom Calling* Amy Sherman describes having been deeply affected by a sermon Tim Keller had preached on Proverbs 11:10: "When the righteous prosper, the city rejoices" (NIV). According to Keller, "the 'righteous' (Hebrew *tsaddiqim*) are the just, the people who follow God's heart and ways and who see everything they have as gifts from God to be stewarded for his purposes. . . . The righteous in the book of Proverbs are by definition those who are willing to disadvantage themselves for the community while the wicked are those who put their own economic, social, and personal needs ahead of the needs of the community."[17] The righteous—that is to say, the church—cause their neighborhoods and cities to rejoice as a result of their glad and generous housekeeping.

In chapter 13, Sherman describes two churches that took seriously the call to be the *tsaddiqim* and liberally shared their resources for the rejoicing of the city. One church adopted a school, improved housing, and pooled its medical and dental expertise to offer free services. Another church dedicated its efforts to both local and global efforts to fight human trafficking. Sherman suggests churches ask themselves these penetrating questions to assess their commitment to generous justice: "Are we engaged in efforts that are relevant to the groans of creation and the cries of the poor? Are we producing disciples whose work is contributing to profound transformations that set people dancing in the streets? Have we joined King Jesus on his grand, sweeping mission of restoration? In cooperation with him, are we bringing foretastes of justice and shalom?"[18] These are questions for the church related to housekeeping. They remind us that we make a home for the wandering lost in our cities not simply by throwing open our church doors but by identifying and attending to their most desperate needs. If we want to sing the stories of home, let's make a real, dry place out of the rain for our closest neighbors.

NEIGHBORS

Much to the dismay of his disciples, Jesus often spoke in parables, obscuring the truth from immediate recognition. But one of Jesus' stories—about neighborliness—seems as easy to understand today as it might have been for its first-century audience. In telling the story of the good Samaritan (Lk 10), Jesus is answering a man who has desired "to justify himself," a man who is interested in ticking the necessary boxes for inheriting eternal reward. Jesus has reminded him that he must obey the law of God, which can be summarized as simply as this: worship and neighborliness.

The man, however, requires further clarification. "Who is my neighbor?" And this question is Jesus' entrée into a story about three men who stumble across what, at first glance, seems to be a corpse. In the street lies a man half-dead—a bleeding victim of armed robbery. The first two men, charged with the haste of priestly work, do not kneel in compassion but hurry past. But the third—a Samaritan, an ethnic pariah—stops. He stoops to tend the stranger's wounds and then gathers him up in his arms, taking him to an inn where he empties his pockets and charges the innkeeper with the stranger's care. "Take care of him, and whatever more you spend, I will repay you when I come back." As Jesus tells the story, it becomes clear that it is not the stranger who is the neighbor but the Samaritan. A neighbor is the one who takes up the housekeeping—or in this case, the considerable cost and inconvenience of compassion.

In late fall of 2017, Grace Toronto Church, as part of our ministry initiative called Grace Center for the Arts, will host a multimedia event that we are calling "Neighbors." As we complete the renovations of our new building, we want to seize the opportune moment for making proper introductions. Currently planned as a concert, an architectural tour, and a photography exhibit of local residents (in addition to the publication of GCA's magazine, *Imprint*), "Neighbors" is one way of opening the conversation—to say that we are glad to be at the corner of Jarvis and Carlton streets and that we want to partner in taking up the city's housekeeping. Most importantly, we hope it affords the opportunity to begin sharing what is central to the gospel: the story of a Father and his welcome. A story of neighbors. A story of home.

Let the light of your housekeeping shine, Jesus told his church. And your city—single and married, childless and child-full—will give glory to the Homemaker.

8

LOVE AND MARRIAGE
The Routine Work of I Do

151 GLENDON AVENUE
TORONTO, ONTARIO

I PULL AROUND THE CORNER. He approaches in his black sedan, wearing his familiar tight-lipped smile that says *I'm happy to see you*. And I am happy to see him, happier still that he is headed to Costco on what has become his regular errand. In a little more than an hour, he'll come home with expertly puzzled and packed boxes, one of which will contain two rotisserie chickens. He, not I, will assume the gruesome task of boning the carcasses because that's what love does: spare the handling of animal flesh.

Ours is a marriage in the middle years, if I can presume the privilege of future decades for having and holding the man I married twenty years ago. We are forty-somethings, knee-deep in life's housekeeping. Children, career, college savings, and caring for our parents preoccupy our thoughts and predict our sudden, usually silent collapse into bed. Life bulges with tedium. We sleep hard. We sign permission slips and buy shoes. I remember to keep bleach under the bathroom sink, and Ryan remembers five-dollar bills for Saturday's allowance. That the family calendar is a labyrinth becomes evident every time I travel to speak. I tape the meal plan inside one of the kitchen cabinets and remind everyone to finish the leftovers. In the cab on the way to the airport, I worry that no one will water the fiddle leaf.

Marriage in the middle years is a cantering horse: you try not to get thrown. But that image, apt for speed, does not convey what is also true about marriage in midlife, which is its monotony. There are fewer new days under the sun after you have been married several decades, and if I'm honest, the sameness can produce boredom. In marriage's middle years we have to find joy in the everyday miracle of keeping our promises. We must keep at the repetitive, routine work of I do. As C. S. Lewis has written, every marriage must, as it matures, "submit to the loss of the thrill . . . [which] will be compensated . . . by a quieter and more lasting kind of interest."[1]

In their book *40/40 Vision*, Peter Greer and Greg Lafferty explore the seeming oppression of midlife's sameness. But they don't give into midlife pessimism. Instead, they encourage readers to see a God who exults in monotony. As part of his cosmic housekeeping, he raises the sun every morning, tucks it in every night. As G. K. Chesterton has written, "[Children] always say, 'Do it again'; and the grown-up person does it again until he is nearly dead. For grown-up people are not strong enough to exult in monotony. But perhaps God is strong enough to exult in monotony. It is possible that God says every morning, 'Do it again' to the sun; and every evening, 'Do it again' to the moon. . . . It may be that he has the eternal appetite of infancy."[2] God is never bored, and maybe one experiment of midlife marriage is choosing his delight in what's predictable and well-worn.

It is easy to tire of the marital housekeeping: confession, forgiveness, clear communication, presumption of innocence, self-sacrifice, even regular sex.[3] Boredom, not lust, was the demise of the central character of Gustave Flaubert's novel *Madame Bovary*. Emma Bovary is tragically sentimental. She chases a beatific vision of the good life, one that existed on the plane of the rapturous rather than the mundane. She marries Charles, a country doctor, in search of a vision of happiness inspired by the novels she read as a young girl. When her marriage fails the standard of romantic fiction, Emma pursues a series of adulterous love affairs; to her chagrin, she finds in adultery "all the platitudes of marriage."[4] Curiously, as a cure for Emma's frivolous nature her mother-in-law prescribes a healthy dose of housekeeping. "'Do you know what your wife needs?' said Madame Bovary to her son. 'She needs some hard work, some manual labour. If she were like nearly everyone else, forced to earn a living, she wouldn't have these vapours of hers, which all come from stuffing her head with nonsense and leading a life of idleness.'"[5]

151 GLENDON AVENUE
TORONTO, ONTARIO

SHE STANDS AT MY DOOR, tearfully recounting how the man she had counted as friend, and even as potential husband, has not returned her phone calls and deliberately avoids running into her at work. Theirs had been a new and easy friendship, and she had let herself hope, even pray, that something more romantic and lasting would develop. Like many of my other unmarried friends, she is in her mid-thirties, caught up in her own cycles of sameness. With me, she wonders aloud when the monotonous, solitary march of the years will end and her history of home begin. I hear in her voice tacit worry about her aging ovaries and her diminishing chances to marry and mother.

"You're just so lucky," she says, casting a glance at all the tangible signs of my housekeeping: family pictures, children's shoes, our large dining room table. I want to concede these gifts guiltily. I nod when she cries and stammers, "I just want to be married."

My friend's long wait for marriage is not anomalous. According to recent sociological research, the marriage rate, 50.5 percent in 2015, is falling in the United States. (At its all-time high in the twentieth century in 1960, 72.2 percent of Americans were married.)[6] The coming-of-age script is changing for women and men in North America as people marry older and have their children later.

While we might rightly bemoan what seems to be the demise of "till death do us part," the church has historically disagreed over the importance of marriage. Early church father Augustine of Hippo favored Paul's preference for celibacy (1 Cor 7:7-8). For centuries the church, while affirming Genesis 2 and the goodness of marriage, conceded the distractions of domestic life. One medieval solution proposed to divide the "housekeeping" among the people of God. Married people would tend to "earth" while monks and nuns, who renounced marriage, would do the work of heaven, praying "*for* the world, in the world's stead."[7]

During the Reformation, theologians like John Calvin and Martin Luther abolished what had become a sacrosanct division between celibates and married. By developing the concept of vocation, they taught that domestic obligation could be rendered as service to God, just as prayer and fasting were forms of worship: "*Everyone* [was] now expected to live all their lives *coram Deo*; before the face of God."[8] At the most fundamental level, vocation became a Christological category—a way of baptizing the housekeeping as sacred duty performed to God in the service of one's neighbor.

Regretfully, the Enlightenment turned us in upon ourselves, replacing religious devotion with romantic love. It has bequeathed to us, even within the church, today's legacy of "family home" as highest good. Romantic ardor has become the substitute for reverent worship, the family home for God's house. As a very public example, Marian Evans, later known as the famous Victorian novelist George Eliot, took a lover in 1854: George Henry Lewes, a married man with whom she lived publicly for more than twenty years. When Eliot met Lewes, his wife had just given birth to her sixth child, three of whom were fathered not by Lewes but by her lover, Thornton Leigh Hunt. Lewes and his wife had initially agreed on an open marriage, and because Lewes had not pursued divorce after the birth of the first illegitimate child, he was prevented from dissolving the marriage later when he met and fell in love with Eliot.

As a young woman George Eliot had eschewed the religious faith of her childhood and felt no compunction to defend her domestic arrangement with Lewes to her own family or to the public. "We are leading no life of self-indulgence," she explained, "except indeed, that being happy in each other, we find everything easy. We are working hard to provide for others better than ourselves, and to fulfill every responsibility that lies upon us. Levity and pride would not be sufficient basis for that."[9] Eliot refused to be disgraced by her unconventional household arrangement. If we have sinned, Eliot defended, our transgression is our happiness. And at least we are keeping up with the world's housekeeping.

Domestic arrangements like Eliot's are hardly extraordinary today, which is one reason it remains important for the church to affirm the goodness of marriage today. An important act of housekeeping is the promise to have and to hold, for better or worse. But if marriage is sacred vocation, it is not our highest calling. And if children are blessings, they are not our greatest gifts.

When heaven meets earth, earthly marriage will cease the moment Christ raises his glass and drinks to his bride, the church.

DREAD OF THE HOUSEKEEPING

Marriage and children, though not the highest forms of home, are nevertheless good gifts. Yet modern women are frequently warned about the costs of domestic housekeeping. Although family life has often been perceived as boon to men's careers, for women, it has come to be regarded, in certain circles, as impediment to professional ambition.[10] In her book *The End of Men: And the Rise of Women*, Hanna Rosin studies the hookup culture of American universities and concludes that it works precisely because ambitious young women are wishing to delay marriage for professional reasons. "Today's college girls likens a serious suitor to an accidental pregnancy in the nineteenth century: a danger to be avoided at all costs, lest it thwart a promising future."[11] Rosin interviewed one woman who at the age of twenty-eight broke off an engagement thirty thousand feet in the air. When the plane experienced serious turbulence, the woman suddenly realized she preferred death to life "in Darien, Connecticut, cooking in the kitchen with kids at her feet."[12]

According to the cultural narrative, the twenty-first-century woman is wisest to reduce the burden of her domestic housekeeping in order to consecrate herself more fully to professional pursuit. If she marries, she should, at the very least, bear fewer children. In a 2013 piece for *The Atlantic* called "The Secret of

Being Both a Successful Writer and a Mother: Have Just One Kid," writer Lauren Sandler cites the illustrious company of women writers who bore and raised just one child: Susan Sontag, Alice Walker, Margaret Atwood, and Joan Didion. In a collection of essays titled "Selfish, Shallow, and Self-Absorbed," edited by Meghan Daum, sixteen writers defend their decision to pursue a childless and oft-perceived "selfish and too-tidy existence."[13] One writer describes her antipathy for the "strange and un-enviable breed" of mothers she'd too often met, describing their manner as "harried, hampered, resentful."[14] Another writer cites the accomplishments she would never have achieved had she tethered herself to the care of a family. No doubt attitudes like these, loathe to carry the added burdens of domestic commit-ments, contribute to the common pity with which I am some-times regarded by perfect strangers: "You have *five* children?"

NECESSARY SELF-SACRIFICE

I confess to my own fears associated with domestic self-sacrifice. With six greedy mouths to feed, I worry it will be a permanent fast for me. I imagine the fish and loaves of my life being gobbled by the crowds, and I doubt the presence of Jesus to ensure a dozen baskets of leftovers. Will giving to my family run the risk of per-sonal bankruptcy? But as Mark Jones, pastor of Faith Vancouver Presbyterian Church and author of *Knowing Christ*, recently taught at our church in Toronto, though we see self-sacrifice and self-fulfillment as two contradictory impulses, the Bible does not support such a view. Ephesians 5:22-33, a classic marriage text, holds up the model of Christ's sacrifice as an example for marriage: "In the same way [as Christ] husbands should love their wives as their own bodies. *He who loves his wife loves himself*" (v. 28, emphasis added). The mystery of self-sacrifice in marriage is that it is not an obstacle to self-fulfillment but a means to it.

This doesn't mean that marriage and motherhood ensure that women get everything they want. In one sense, every family is a finite pie, and embodiment and emplacement are inherent limitations. The family as a whole does not have infinite stores of energy and time, and the family coffers must be shared. When my husband, Ryan, spent eight years of evenings and Saturdays poring over stacks of index cards to prepare for his actuarial exams, I shouldered the bulk of childcare and housework. When he then decided to pursue a graduate degree, I continued supporting him (although not always as happily as I might have wished). But as Ryan would now gratefully acknowledge, his professional ambitions were, in part, made possible by my willingness to waylay my own.

My sacrifices for Ryan's professional success aren't the only sacrifices of our marriage, however. Ryan has assumed burdens for our family that I haven't: financial responsibility, as an example. With five children to feed and a writer-wife to support, his dreams of starting a small business or getting a PhD have also suffered small deaths. He won't take the cross-country move he has been offered because he refuses to uproot our family again. He'll frequently bail on after-work schmooze sessions, coming home to dinner with us instead. Every time he lays down his own life, he affirms his love for me. And strangely, he also loves himself.

In his essay "Feminism, the Body, and the Machine," Wendell Berry responds to reader outrage over a previously published essay in which he admitted that his wife types his manuscripts. When feminists cried foul, in his characteristically wry way, Berry admitted, "My offense is that I am a man who receives some help from his wife."[15]

"Marriage, in what is evidently its most popular version," writes Berry, "is now on the one hand an intimate 'relationship' involving (ideally) two successful careerists in the same bed, and on the other hand a sort of private political system in which rights and interests must be constantly asserted and defended. Marriage, in other words, has now taken the form of divorce: a prolonged and impassioned negotiation as to how things shall be divided."[16] He continues: "What appears to infuriate [the feminists] the most is their supposition that [my wife] works for nothing. They assume—and this is the orthodox assumption of the industrial economy—that the only help worth giving is not given at all, but sold."[17]

According to Berry, in modern marriage we don't give and take: we borrow and repay—which is to say we've traveled far from the biblical ideal of marriage as described for us in Ephesians 5, where wives and husbands lay themselves down for each other's flourishing. The mystery of marriage isn't its limitless capacity for securing our personal happiness. The mystery of marriage is its witness to the eternal, self-sacrificing love of Jesus for his bride, whom he intends to purify and present holy and blameless, without spot or wrinkle. As the apostle Paul argued, marriage points beyond itself to a greater reality: "I am saying that it refers to Christ and the church" (Eph 5:32).

BIBLICAL MARRIAGE

In his book *Scripture and the Authority of God*, N. T. Wright details how we as Christians might read the Scriptures more faithfully, and in the final two chapters he employs his hermeneutic in two case studies, one of which addresses the subject of monogamy.

It will seem strange, perhaps, that Wright chooses to tackle a subject about which there is so little disagreement. But this is exactly Wright's point. If we were reading the Scriptures most objectively, we might wonder more about the prevalence of polygamy in the Old Testament. What biblical evidence do we have that monogamous marriage is better than polygamous marriage? "I suspect," he writes, "it is only the social context in the Western world that has stopped more people from re-marking on [the Bible's remarkable silence on polygamy]," sug-gesting that our "biblical" views of marriage might not be so biblical after all.[18]

Reading Wright's chapter "The Case for Monogamy" inter-ested me in the polygamous marriages of King David and the scandals of the royal harem. I understand that these aren't typical texts for exploring marriage, and I don't suggest that they are prescriptive in any way. However, to believe that all Scripture is given for our good is to affirm that these passages can illuminate truths about human nature, about marriage, even about the reasons all of us should be looking for a greater home than the one we might be privileged to make with a husband or wife and our children.

MICHAL

Michal is the first woman to marry the young shepherd boy David, before his ascent to the throne of Israel. Despite that the biblical text mentions twice that Michal loves David (and this, the *only* mention of a woman loving a man in the Old Tes-tament), her courtship to the ruddy and handsome youngest son of Jesse is not a romantic fairytale but a story of political intrigue. In fact, Michal's marriage comes early in the David narrative when the storyteller is much keener to portray the public David than the private man. What little we do know is that Saul has trumped up a plan to exact his murderous jealousy on the man whose slain tens of thousands are winning him public acclaim. Saul will give his daughter in marriage to David in order to seal a political alliance and keep David under his royal thumb, naming a considerable bride price: one hundred Philistine foreskins.

David pays the price and marries Michal, but his relationship with Saul sours again quickly. Multiple times, Saul seeks to avenge his jealous wrath; multiple times, David escapes. In one early account in 1 Samuel 19, Michal creates an elaborate ruse for helping David escape the messengers Saul sends to kill him. Saul, seeing opportunity to break the ties with David, gives Michal to another man: Palti, son of Laish.

Seven or eight years of silence suspend between David's narrow escape and Michal's reappearance, as political pawn, in the David narrative (2 Sam 3:12-16). Saul and his son Jonathan are dead; Abner, commander of Saul's army, has surrendered to David and pledged to him his fealty. David, fully recognized King of Israel, wants Michal back. Like so many other biblical women, Michal's life changes, in a moment, at the whim of men, and the road to Jerusalem, paved with her powerlessness, is littered with memories of another life, another home, and another man's bed. As perhaps one of the most palpably tragic episodes of the biblical narrative, her husband, Paltiel, trails behind her, weeping for the wife he is losing (2 Sam 3:15-16).[19]

The next time Michal speaks, she erupts with seething anger (2 Sam 6:16-23). If Michal has ever loved David, she now despises him. The text indicates her indignation over his immodest dancing and dress when he has paraded with the people toward Jerusalem, where David intends to install the ark of the Lord. David has been a magnanimous host at the day's festivities, and every household has left with their hands full of bread and meat and dried raisins. But when David finally returns to bless his own household, he is met with hostility rather than welcome. "How the king of Israel honored himself today," Michal sneers sarcastically, jeering that David has made a public fool of himself. But she, the woman, is not to have the last word; the king speaks, and her barren silence follows. "I shall be held in honor," he retorts. The story concludes with Michal's curse: "And Michal the daughter of Saul had no child to the day of her death" (2 Sam 6:23). We don't hear from the barren Michal again.

There is a great cultural chasm between Michal's story and ours, and yet it remains true today that married life, for all of us, heads in directions we don't expect. Each of us stands at the altar and pronounces our vows with incredible naiveté. The years will change us, and they will change our David. Perhaps we meet with unexpected financial difficulty or a life-altering diagnosis. Whatever the surprise, the question is always before us: What can we make of the marriage we have, even if it might never be the marriage we dreamed of?

There is too much silence in Michal's story to understand the root cause of her anger toward David, but it is not at all unlikely that it has accrued interest over the years, a reminder that forgiveness in marriage must be an everyday act of housekeeping— and with it, repentance. In marriage "I'm sorry" is just as important as "I do." To keep house in marriage, we have to keep choosing love's bearing, love's believing, love's hoping, and love's enduring all things (1 Cor 13:7).

Michal and many others do not get their happily ever after. Yet even then it is ours to cherish the promise of Isaiah 54:5: "For your Maker is your husband, / the LORD of hosts is his name." When marriage fails to satisfy our deepest longings for home, we can remember our greater Groom.

ABIGAIL

After his escape from Saul, having left Michal behind, David travels with a band of six hundred foot soldiers. Provisions are scarce, and as we see in 1 Samuel 25, David depends on the good will of neighbors for feeding his small army. In the chapter just prior, David has mercifully spared Saul's life, but if David has resisted violent overthrow of Saul's government, in 1 Samuel 25 he appears eerily bloodthirsty. He has asked for food provisions from Nabal, whose household is festively celebrating the annual sheep shearing event. However, Nabal has rudely refused him, ignoring the good will David and his men have shown to his shepherds and flock, and dismissing David as a public nuisance rather than an anointed king. "Every man strap on his sword!" David cries, vowing to leave none of Nabal's household alive.

Enter Abigail: the beautiful, decisive, discerning wife of the man named "Fool." The servants anticipate David's anger at Nabal's refusal, and they quickly explain the situation to Abigail, whose judgment they explicitly trust. The narrative emphasizes Abigail's haste in response. Quickly devising a plan, Abigail sends ahead the provisions that have already been prepared for the feast (meat, wine, bread, and cakes), which she knows Nabal has already refused to share. And when she meets David and his four hundred marauding men, what seems implicit in the text is that the gifts have been sent ahead but have not been received. David's anger is not assuaged, and he continues his plan of assault until Abigail dismounts her donkey and falls at his feet (1 Sam 25:23).

Abigail admits the household's wrong, but she also admits Nabal's worthlessness. Perhaps most importantly, she invokes the name of Yahweh seven times, warning David against unnecessary bloodguilt and reminding him of his rightful claim to the throne. Her courage is unmistakable—both because she has defied her husband, whom the text describes as "harsh and badly behaved" and also because she has thrown herself into the path of soldiers bent on revenge. David praises her wisdom and haste, and when it is later reported that Nabal has died (seemingly as consequence of his sin), David sends for Abigail to become his wife.

We cannot know if David "fell in love" with the brave woman at his feet that day or if he took her into his harem as an act of justice, sparing her the economic misfortune that widowhood was in ancient culture. But we do know that Abigail effectively disappears from the narrative with the exception of one story, in which Ziklag (the Philistine city where David has sought refuge from Saul) is raided and burned, and David's wives and children (including Abigail) have been carried off as plunder. Abigail, who survived the harshness of Nabal, who was kindly treated by David, is now possibly a victim of one of the oldest strategies of war: rape.

Violence isn't just an incidence of war or depraved city streets: it happens within committed domestic partnerships, even marriage. Although theologian Scot McKnight had been Ruth Tucker's colleague at Trinity International University for many years, he did not know that Tucker, author of eighteen books, including the most recently published *Black and White Bible, Black and Blue Wife*, was systematically abused by her pastor husband. On his blog McKnight describes his shock at discovering the secrets of her violent marriage. "As I read this book," McKnight writes on his blog, "I kept thinking this: (1) How could this all be going on without our knowing it? and (2) abuse lives undercover all the time."[20]

Abigail was a victim of sexual violence in war, and it's not a stretch to also imagine her a victim of Nabal's cruelty. Her story calls to mind the present-day terror of women living in fear of their husbands, who are ill-advised that the marital housekeeping involves remaining in harm's way. A biblical marriage is not an abusive one, and a godly husband never raises his hand. As one pastor has written very clearly, "God not only hates divorce, but also the one whose garment is covered with violence (Mal. 2:16). A violent and abusive man has broken the marriage covenant by his sinful choices; he is the 'divorcer,' and that marriage is not honoring to the Lord (1 Cor. 7:15)."[21] For women facing threat at the hands of their husband, they should look for help and safety in their wider family, the church. They should also call the police.

BATHSHEBA

There are other wives in David's royal harem beside Michal and Abigail: Bathsheba is a woman whose agency is stolen when her beauty is noticed from the king's rooftop. Called to a king's bed, bereaved twice by a king's sin, she is a silent spectator until it becomes necessary to fight for her son Solomon's rightful claim to the throne. But when she is granted audience with David many years later, he is in bed with the younger, more beautiful Abishag, whose work is keeping the king warm. If the wife of Uriah (as Bathsheba is so often called) had once been David's favored wife, at least favored enough to secure the king's oath that her son would rule over Israel after his death, at this point in the narrative she has aged. Her breasts sag. And David's courtiers know that she cannot give to her husband the pleasure the smooth-skinned, bosomy Abishag can. Bathsheba is not the young beauty she once was. And this is her grief—one that many of us know as we look in the mirror.

When our anniversary rolled around last August, Ryan surprised me with plane tickets to New York City. We left weeks later, and somewhere between Midtown and the Bronx, I let go of the interminable list of household to-dos and began enjoying myself. For several days Ryan and I prowled Manhattan's streets. We walked the High Line and the Brooklyn Bridge, found a pizzeria and devoured two large pizzas together. I towed Ryan through the Period Rooms at the Met, and at the Cloisters we learned about polychromatic medieval statuary by an art historian.

On our final day we watched tennis till the sky turned black. If I am still admiring the man I married twenty years ago, if we are still finding things to talk about, if there is continued pleasure in sharing our bodies with each other, can this be a small thing?

I know it's no small thing when the phone rings, and I answer a call from an acquaintance. "I'm getting a divorce," she says. In one way it is strange that she confides to me, a practical stranger, her intimate grief. In another way it seems to be the most natural thing in the world. When we bleed, we look to cauterize the wound. And that's what divorce seems to be: in its rising action and climax and dénouement, horror of an enduring kind. "Churches all agree with one another about marriage a great deal more than any of them agrees with the outside world," wrote C. S. Lewis. "They all regard divorce as something like cutting up a living body as a kind of surgical operation."[22] God hates divorce, and I begin to understand why.

Marriage isn't everything. It isn't our best home or final hope. Nevertheless, it is worth the routine work of "I do." After all, marriage is its own kind of stability. Though Ryan and I may never forge a permanent connection to a city, we have the permanence of the vows we pronounced to each other on a mild August day in 1996. These vows keep something in place. They protect us from our own wandering restlessness. Perhaps the most beautiful of marriage chapters, best suited for public reading at every wedding ceremony, is not Ephesians 5 but 1 Corinthians 15:51: "Behold! I tell you a mystery. We shall not all sleep, but we shall all be changed." Kept promises—to have and to hold until death—give testimony not to the powers of human love but to the faithfulness of the greater Groom.

Which doesn't make it less important but more, to keep up the marital housekeeping.

Genesis 15

Heifer, goat, and ram,
full-grown man and full-grown woman,
we lay with the animals in the hot sun.
This green earth and blue sky,
the grass around our ears:
breastbone and sternum
wishbones.
The crowd has gathered for the oblation,
to witness the cleaving and cleaving,
the covenant—
"Let me swear now:
Tear me apart in kind,"
split me in two;
cleave me . . .
Tear me apart
rip my soul from my body
slice my joints from my marrow,
if we—Man and Woman—are torn in two:
if I betray this covenant . . . [23]

9

SAYING GRACE

Feasting Together

177 DAWLISH AVENUE
TORONTO, ONTARIO

WE INVITED TWENTY-ONE PEOPLE for Easter our first year in Toronto, worrying, only after the invitations had been sent, where to seat everyone. The first floor of our rented 1920s colonial consisted of a galley kitchen, modest dining and living rooms, and a small porch that had been converted into an office. There was hardly room for a party.

On the eve of the gathering we moved the microwave to the basement, adding another foot of usable counter space in the kitchen. We planned an outdoor egg hunt and prayed for good weather. When the guests arrived, we sat four teenagers around a small table in the converted porch: two on the love seat, one on the swivel office chair, and the fourth on a folding chair. We crammed the youngest kids in the basement with paper plates (and closed the door at the top of the stairs). Eight adults politely managed their elbows in the dining room, and before anything was served, we bowed to acknowledge our gratitude, saying grace for the food, the friends, and the feast. *Our Father.*

If furniture were a financial portfolio, we are heavily invested in tables. Years ago, when our family lived in Ohio, two friends and I headed east in the pre-dawn hours for Freeburg, Pennsylvania, where I'd found a drop leaf table at a small furniture outlet. "Tea table for 2, dining table for 8," the website had read. Two tanks of gas later, the dowry was paid, and the pencil-legged Shaker table was added to the household harem.

Her slim figure assumed its place alongside other tables: the Target pedestal table, bought on clearance and scarred by an exploding whiteout pen, a table that has performed kitchen duty but now stages Lego battles in the boys' bedroom; two rectangular tables purchased from Craigslist, site of puzzles and sewing projects and overflow dinner seating for sticky-fingered children; my grandmother's oak drop-leaf table, beautiful and blond, curvaceous in leg; and finally, our extrawide, extralong dining room table, which comfortably seats our family of seven and can be expanded to accommodate sixteen. Altogether, we have table capacity for seating fifty-six people for dinner. (I have never attempted such madness.)

Our tables are our most important furniture, eating so important a part of our family life that it is not unusual for one of my children to ask, as I tuck him into bed, "What's for breakfast tomorrow?" At my mother's invitation when I was a child, I developed an easy familiarity in the kitchen. Family dinner was a quotidian event, and holidays were occasions to feast. I watched my mother and grandmother and my great-aunt Pauline, in the days leading up to Thanksgiving and Christmas and Easter, dedicate hours to peeling potatoes and apples, washing and salting and basting the turkey, pinching dough and forming homemade rolls. They pulled a chair up to the counter, and on it I stood tall enough to help them. Whatever emotional depth might have lacked in my family as I was growing up, we more than made up for in food.

In my first clumsy year of motherhood, our household GDP (and my relative productivity) could have been measured by the output of loaf pans and muffin tins. I baked bread. And baked it daily. I had watched my mother muscle dough, swiftly turning and folding and kneading the floured mound. When her arms tired, she would call my father to finish, and when my brother and I got older, we too were enlisted in the dusty business, made most worthwhile when the dough had risen to the rim of the buttered bowl and we were permitted the delicious violence of punching it down. As a new mother I had no sure-footedness about parenting, but at the very least I knew what to do in the kitchen.

Food has now become our family's easiest means of welcome. It's not always dinner that our guests show up for, although if they time it right, we'll find them a seat. Sometimes they're coming for a cup of coffee, even pouring it themselves. Always, they're eager for the kind of slow, intentional conversation that happens around a table, never the television. They want to know and be known. Twenty years and five children later, I continue to cook: in part because people are perpetually hungry, but mostly because I believe the table is a burning bush. Around the feast we are enflamed with the presence of God.

In Scripture the meal has holy significance. Heaven itself is pictured as a wedding feast.

TABLE LIFE

In Don Freeman's classic picture book, Corduroy is a small stuffed bear that lives in the toy department of a local store. Corduroy is

missing a button from his overalls, a fact he's only made aware of
when, early in the story, a little girl begs her mother to buy him.
"I've spent too much already," the mother refuses. "Besides, he
doesn't look new. He's lost the button to one of his shoulder straps."[1]

When the store closes that night, Corduroy goes in search of
a replacement button, a journey that requires a harrowing ride
up the escalator. On the second floor, in the mattress department,
the little bear finds what he thinks will work for the repair.
However, although he tugs at a button on one of the mattresses
and eventually loosens it, the *pop!* of the button sends him
crashing into a tall floor lamp, which topples and tumbles to the
ground with Corduroy.

"Now who in the world did that?" the night watchman exclaims, taking his flashlight and searching the store. "Somebody
must be hiding around here!" The guard finds Corduroy, puts
him under his arm, and replaces him on his proper shelf in the
toy department. The next day the little girl, Lisa, returns with
money she has saved from her piggy bank. Refusing a box, she
buys Corduroy and carries her new friend back home to her
apartment. The room is pictured with a chair, a chest of drawers,
a girl-sized bed, and a bed sized just for Corduroy.

"This must be home," Corduroy says. "I *know* I've always
wanted a home."[2]

There isn't a table in Lisa's bedroom-become-home, but the
story of Corduroy reminds us of the material dimensions of
home. On the one hand, Corduroy's new home isn't his new
chair, the chest of drawers, and the bed. On the other, each
piece of furniture signals the welcoming love of a little girl for
her bear. In the same way, in the home that God has made and
is remaking for his people, the furniture isn't what makes for
welcome. Nevertheless, a table has a central, cherished place in
the kingdom of God.

It's God's food that says welcome.

God has a long history of feeding his people. He fed Adam and Eve from the trees of the garden. He fed wandering Israel with honey flakes that fell from the sky. And finally he sent his own Son, calling him the Bread of Life. As the psalmists write, we are all sojourners and guests at God's table: we feed from his hand. Even Paul, in his sermon at Lystra, speaks of the witness God left for himself in "satisfying [our] hearts with food and gladness" (Acts 14:17).

Our redemption story is bound up with the housekeeping of a table. In our homes we keep the feast by offering God's welcome to others: not only family and friends, Jesus said, but the needy stranger (Mt 25:35-36). Around our tables we feed Christ himself, and our shared feast-keeping is sure measure of our love for him. In our churches we keep the feast every time we drink the blood and eat the body of Jesus Christ, proclaiming his death until he comes. But feast-keeping isn't only the temporary business of earth. We will also keep the feast in heaven, especially to mark the occasion of our homecoming, which Jesus himself looked forward to on the night of Passover before his arrest and crucifixion: "I have earnestly desired to eat this Passover with you before I suffer. For I tell you I will not eat it until it is fulfilled in the kingdom of God" (Lk 22:15-16). To be a Christian is to keep the feast.

DOING THE DISHES

Feast-keeping involves the unglamorous work of housekeeping, which may be one reason too few of us commit ourselves to it. Personally, I have tired of sermons about the two sisters of Lazarus, based on Luke 10:38-42, that scandalize Martha and venerate Mary. Of course, Martha needn't have been "anxious" or "troubled" about the details of the meal she was preparing for Jesus, his disciples, and her family. To be sure, she needed reminding that the meal wasn't the *end* but the *means*. But she isn't only to be condemned. For all her unholy franticness, Martha was faithfully keeping the feast. If Jesus, the disciples, Lazarus, and his two sisters were to enjoy a meal together, crowded around a table, someone needed to get to the grocery store, stir the simmering soup, and set out spoons and bowls. That work wasn't better than sitting at Jesus' feet, but it was nonetheless necessary.

If consumer trends told the truth, North Americans would be an extraordinarily hospitable people. The size of the modern kitchen has grown in recent decades, and we are spending more and more on the tools of our domestic trade. For those who can afford to shop stores such as Williams-Sonoma and Sur la Table, an array of high-end kitchen gadgetry is available for purchase: Shun knives, Breville toasters, Viking ranges, and Sub-Zero refrigerators. For those of us on stricter budgets, we have no fewer options at big box stores such as Bed, Bath & Beyond and Target, whose aisles teem with items for outfitting the kitchen and home.

But as Megan McArles writes in her article for the *Atlantic*, "The Joy of Not Cooking," we are not cooking at nearly the rate of our grandmothers and great-grandmothers despite our expensive ceramic Dutch ovens and immersion blenders. McArles notes that her grandmother, making do with battered Revere Ware and a mishmash of rusty tools, cooked three square meals a day, canned her own fruit and preserves, and served homemade dessert at every lunch and dinner. In the 1920s the average woman spent approximately thirty hours a week in the kitchen. By the 1950s, that figure had dropped to twenty hours. Today, women aren't likely to spend more than 5.5 hours a week in the kitchen, which begs the question: Why are we spending so much money on a room of the house we largely ignore? Jack Schwefel, the

CEO of Sur La Table, explains that consumers will pay $349.95 for the Margaritaville Frozen Concoction Maker because they "picture themselves outside by the pool, surrounded by 20 of their friends."[3] We are sold on a particular vision of home—one without the housekeeping. We substitute consumption for something more substantive—in this case, biblical feast-keeping. But a table laden with God's feast does not have to be Pinterest perfect; it need not impress. It will, however, require guests and elbows, even a fair degree of sweat.

That feast-keeping, even eating, is *work* is something I was reminded of when rereading Rachel Marie Stone's important book *Eat with Joy*. In her chapter titled "Restorative Eating," she argues that keeping company at a table is as convalescent an activity as dunking in the stirred waters at the biblical pool of Bethesda. "Meals together are a wonderful 'treatment' for boredom and loneliness, especially for the elderly and those who live alone; they can also stave off eating disorders."[4] Anorexia nervosa, which kills nearly 20 percent of its sufferers, is the most lethal of all mental illnesses, but, surprisingly, one proven, effective treatment for the disease is called "family-based therapy/ treatment" or FBT. "Under the guidance of a doctor, a nutritionist and a Maudsley-sympathetic counselor, you sit down for three meals and two snacks a day with your anorexic loved one and *eat with them*."[5]

Stone explores the work involved for both patient and parent in FBT. One anorexic patient finds the act of eating too laborious: she would rather be fed through a feeding tube. Parents committed to helping their anorexic daughters describe the endless hours of meal planning and preparation, not to mention the unhurried company they commit to keeping around the table. Meals are work to prepare, even work to eat. And they always leave dishes to do. It's the housekeeping of feast-keeping

that these families discover on the journey toward healing—
which is work all God's people are called to.

THE JEWISH HISTORY OF FEAST

When Moses, at the ripe age of eighty, is commanded by God
to lead his people out of Egypt, the new nation instituted the
Passover Feast on the eve of their miraculous deliverance. This
feast wasn't merely another event on the religious timetable: it
was occasion for throwing out the old ways of keeping time and
inaugurating a new calendar (Ex 12:2). From the food the Israelites prepared—roasted lamb, unleavened bread, bitter herbs—
to their manner of eating—"in haste," with fastened belts,
strapped sandals, and staff in hand—this meal was a material
means for remembering, even reenacting God's acts of salvation
and narrating the miraculous story to future generations (Ex
12:26-27). Their story had smell and taste.

Although arguably the most important feast of the Jewish calendar, the Passover wasn't the only consecrated feast day of the
year. In Leviticus 23 seven religious feasts, festivals, and fasts are
mentioned: Sabbath, as a weekly event; Passover, the Feast of
Firstfruits, the Feast of Weeks, the Feast of Trumpets, the Day of
Atonement, and the Feast of Booths, as annual events. Moses
describes each of these as "appointed feasts" and "holy convoca-
tions," signaling that they were not private celebrations but national holidays. For three of the feasts (the Feasts of Firstfruits,
the Feast of Weeks, and the Feast of Booths) attendance was
required in Jerusalem, where families presented the required sacrifices and offerings. Elbow to elbow at the table, God's people
recounted in chorus the history of his faithfulness.

I imagine some showing up, like Hannah in 1 Samuel,
wearied or worried or wasted by grief, wondering how to
worship as the internal black clouds gathered and threatened

storm. But the calendar, not the mood, deemed it the right day for *worship*, and maybe for some, when the "pleasing aromas" of the food sacrifices reached their nostrils (after it had reached God's), their countenance lifted and their gladness was restored. Regular feast-keeping can be an antidote to life's episodic turbulence.

In Joel's prophecy, food is cause for joy, privation cause for sadness. God's judgment against Israel is enacted on the fields and the vineyards:

> The fields are destroyed,
>   the ground mourns,
> because the grain is destroyed,
>   the wine dries up,
>   the oil languishes. . . .
> Pomegranate, palm, and apple,
>   all the trees of the field are dried up,
> and gladness dries up
>   from the children of man. (Joel 1:10, 12)

Likewise, when redemption is announced, it is proclaimed in terms of food provision:

> The mountains shall drip sweet wine,
>   and the hills shall flow with milk,
> and all the streambeds of Judah
>   shall flow with water. (Joel 3:18)

These delicious predictions aren't exclusive to Joel. Predominant as a theme across the major and minor prophets is salvation framed not as something conceptual or abstract, but as something sensory and delectable. God has always been the faithful giver of grain, wine, and oil (Hos 2:8). After exile, when Israel is restored to home, the feast will be renewed.

Of the many failures we often cite about ancient Israel, we talk too little of their failure to feast. In the biblical record the Israelites only very occasionally observe the Passover. The first Passover was celebrated the first time in Egypt and the second time in the wilderness. In the forty years of wandering we have no record of Passover celebrations. At the end of the forty years, however, as the Israelites prepared to enter the land flowing with milk and honey, Joshua proclaimed the third occasion for observing the Passover, and the timing of the feast was serendipitous. On day fifteen of the month of Abib, when the sun rose, no manna was found or gathered after morning's dew had fallen. Rather, the people ate the produce of the land (Josh 5:11-12).

When the monarchy was established by the prophet Samuel, no king until the young King Josiah called for the observance of the Passover. David, king after God's own heart, did not observe the Passover feast. Solomon, king of wisdom, failed to commemorate their deliverance from Egypt. Only King Josiah, after having read aloud the long-misplaced copy of the Law, rends his clothes and commands the people to keep the feast (2 Kings 23:21-23). If Israel's sins were amnesiac, if they often forgot the works of God, as the psalmist writes (Ps 78:7), was it because they failed to feast as God had commanded? Was food and its pleasures, the table and its company, meant for securing their obedience? If they had passed the salt, recounting between bites the history of God's demonstrable grace and goodness, wouldn't faith have been fed?

We might ask what's missing materially from our own worship practices, which tend, in Western Protestantism, toward the cerebral rather than the embodied. Are we feeding the hungry of our neighborhoods and cities? Do we share regular meals together with people in our worshiping communities? Do those meals provide opportunities for noticing and celebrating God's work in our midst? And for that matter, do our families routinely prioritize dinner at the table? In other words, is feast-keeping given the priority of more standard spiritual disciplines like prayer and Bible reading?

The Bible, though a primary means of our formation, is not the only one: God has also given us the feast.

THE LORD'S SUPPER

According to his book *Ancient Christian Worship*, Yale Divinity professor Andrew B. McGowan indicates that "the central act around or within which other [acts like] preaching, prayer and prophecy were arranged" was the feast.[6] In the earliest centuries following the resurrection of Christ, churches did not assemble in large buildings but in private homes, and the church potluck was officially born in these homes.

In *Ancient Christian Worship* McGowan describes the ways these meals, referred to sometimes as the Eucharist, the "breaking of the bread," or *agape* (love feast), were similar and dissimilar to the ancient Greco-Roman banquet. Unlike the banquets known to their contemporaries, the Christian meal did not feature the flesh of sacrificed animals. As Justin Martyr writes in the second century, making a defense of Christian practice to the Roman emperor, "We praise [God], to the best of our ability, through prayer and thanksgiving [*eucharistia*] for all we have been given to eat, as we have been taught is the only honor worthy of him; not to consume by fire what he has created for our sustenance, but to use it for ourselves and those in need."[7] At these early meals Christians gave thanks for the food, which they ate and also made sure to share with the hungry. The early Christians weren't carnivorous in their feasting practices, as the Greeks and Romans were. Instead, their meals most prominently featured bread and wine.[8]

The wine did flow generously at early Christian meals, as it did at Greco-Roman banquets, the most famous of which were the philosophical feasts of Plato. At these feasts, after the food was served, the drinking course, or the *symposion*, began, heralding the beginning of protracted conversation. Similarly, at early Christian meals, as the meal finished, a purposeful time of singing and reading began. As Tertullian describes of a typical Christian meal in North Africa in AD 200:

> We do not recline until we have first tasted of prayer to God; as much is eaten as to satisfy the hungry; only as much is drunk as is proper to the chaste. They are satisfied as those who remember that they have to praise God even in the night; they talk as those who know that the Lord is listening. After water for washing the hands, and lights, each is invited to sing publicly to God as able from holy scripture or from their own ability; thus how each has drunk is put to the test. Similarly prayer closes the feast.[9]

If the Christians were sometimes accused of being cannibalistic, feasting on the body of the Lord, according to Tertullian's words they were not to be taken for drunkards. Their dinners together, though hardly somber affairs, were also serious in purpose; they understood feast as central to *formation*.

Feasting was (and continues to be) central to the life of the Christian because it was central to the life of our Lord. In Luke, Jesus is often pictured as someone's dinner guest. In Luke 5 he is invited to the home of Levi, the tax collector, and crowded around Levi's table are the religious dropouts. Jesus' perceived moral laxity at dinnertime inspires the Pharisees to grumble at the disciples, "Why do you eat and drink with tax collectors and sinners?" (v. 30). In Luke 7 Jesus accepts an invitation by a Pharisee, and when they recline at table, a "sinful" woman bathes Jesus' feet with her tears. Her intimate touch is cause for the Pharisee's tacit reproach, though Jesus in turn criticizes the hospitality of his host—and his housekeeping failures. "Do you see this woman? I entered your house; you gave me no water for my feet, but she has wet my feet with her tears and wiped them with her hair. You gave me no kiss, but from the time I came in she has not ceased to kiss my feet. You did not anoint my head with oil, but she has anointed my feet with ointment" (vv. 44-46). In Luke 19 we see Jesus invite himself for lunch at the home of Zacchaeus, a chief tax collector and man chiefly despised by the Jewish people for his greedy collaboration with the Romans. As one scholar has said, "Jesus was killed because of the way he ate."[10]

Jesus was a frequent diner at the homes of other people—so frequent that he was accused of being a glutton and a drunkard. But he was also a frequent host. When a crowd of five thousand men is seated on a hillside near Bethsaida, Jesus spreads a feast from a little boy's lunch, multiplying five loaves and two fish to extravagantly feed the gathered hungry. Twelve baskets of leftovers are retrieved by his disciples after everyone has eaten to his fill. Several chapters later, before Jesus tells the most famous of his parables in Luke 15, he is accused by the religious leaders of his day of "receiving" sinners, not simply eating with them (Lk 15:2). Jesus' crime is his liberal hospitality, which was his embodied way of declaring that God's aching desire is to have company at his table. "Go out to the highways and hedges and compel people to come in, that my house may be filled" (Lk 14:23).

But of all the feasts Jesus participated in, either as guest or host, the most important was the Last Supper, shared with his disciples before his imminent arrest. In the oldest of texts that describe this meal, the apostle Paul explains the holy significance of the bread and wine Jesus and his disciples ate and drank in their borrowed room.

> For I received from the Lord what I also delivered to you,
> that the Lord Jesus on the night when he was betrayed took
> bread, and when he had given thanks, he broke it and said,
> "This is my body which is for you. Do this in remembrance
> of me." In the same way also he took the cup, after supper,
> saying, "This cup is the new covenant in my blood. Do this,
> as often as you drink it, in remembrance of me." For as
> often as you eat this bread and drink the cup, you proclaim
> the Lord's death until he comes. (1 Cor 11:23-26)

As we gather around the table of Communion, we remember the
cross and anticipate the cloud on which Jesus will triumphantly
return. At the table of his supper, we proclaim the gospel of home.

The feast preaches.

Formation and proclamation weren't the only reasons to
keep the feast. Justice was also central to the housekeeping of
God's people. We see this concern demonstrated in Paul's defense of the hungry poor in the Corinthian congregations. The
Corinthian love feasts had become self-preoccupied, for when
they assembled together, everyone ate the food they had individually brought. It was not the Lord's Supper but everyone's
"own meal" (1 Cor 11:21). And just as the manner of eating
today symbolizes status (farm-fresh, organic, free-range, grain-
fed, all descriptors of how the wealthy eat), so in the ancient
world, socioeconomic divisions were visible at the table—sadly,
even at the Lord's Table in Corinth. This cannot be, Paul de-
cries! "One goes hungry, another gets drunk. What! Do you
not have houses to eat and drink in? Or do you despise the
church of God and humiliate those who have nothing?" (1 Cor
11:21-22). To feast on the one body and blood given for the
sustenance of the world and then forget the world's hungry is
anathema to the gospel. The invitations of this kingdom go out

to the most marginalized: "Go out quickly to the streets and lanes of the city, and bring in the poor and crippled and blind and lame!" (Lk 14:21). This is what God, the cosmic host, has commanded. He does not will that any go hungry, and as we pray the prayer that he has taught us to pray, we remember his desire to feed the world. Give *us* this day, *our* daily bread.

The early church consistently demonstrated concern for the hungry in their feast-keeping—from Paul and his chastisement of the Corinthians in the first century to the practice of Eucharist morning gatherings in the fourth, when a remainder of food from the meals was kept and distributed to the needy members of the community. Christian benevolence was not a culturally learned philanthropy; the generous and fair distribution of food was owed to the nature of the Lord's feast. There simply isn't a way to take the bread and cup of Jesus, eating and drinking his body, and ignore one's disadvantaged brothers and sisters across the table. As William Cavanaugh writes in his book *Being Consumed: Economics and Christian Desire*, the Lord's Supper proclaims a different economic and eschatological story than the capitalist narrative. "One story that the market tells is that of scarcity miraculously turned into abundance by consumption itself, a contemporary loaves and fishes saga. . . . The Eucharist tells another story about hunger and consumption. It does not begin with scarcity [because Jesus is the bread of life]."[11] At the Lord's Table, everyone feasts, rich and poor alike.

> O, God,
> Bless this food we are about to receive.
> Give bread to those who are hungry
> And make we who have bread
> To hunger for justice. [12]

KIGALI, RWANDA

We travel the winding roads in a small van, and the terraced hills rise around us. In the valleys, women and children bend at the waist, cultivating the soil by hand. They tend rice and corn and sugar cane, storing the harvest in burlap sacks, which they strap precariously to their bicycles or balance in basins on their heads. It has been more than twenty years since the 1994 genocide, and Rwanda, under the both celebrated and hated leadership of President Paul Kagame, is flourishing. There are armed guards on the street corners of the capital city, but there is also relative peace.

My oldest daughter, Audrey, and I traveled to Rwanda in the summer of 2015 with HOPE International, which, in partnership with Urwego Opportunity Bank and a vast network of local church leaders, has brought microlending and micro-savings services as well as biblically based business training to the residents of Rwanda. We visited some of the small groups benefitting from HOPE's work and listened to clients detail the improvements they had made to their lives and businesses as a result of a microloan.

"I bought a house and land. I have a bike. Now there are cows at my house."

"I have two sheep and employ two people on my farm. I am able to pay the school fees for my two children."

"I have three children, and their names mean 'Gift from God,' 'I will be helped by God,' and 'God helps.' We have a phone and a mattress, and we love to pray."

"We now have electricity. My kids drink milk. The manure from my cow fertilizes my fields. Now I can pray."

But there was one particular woman Audrey and I will never forget. "I was once a woman who was happily married, but I became a widow because of the history of this country," Beatha told us as the light of the afternoon faded. The middle-age

Rwandan woman recounted firsthand horrors of the 1994 genocide. She described the day the Interahamwe, a Hutu paramilitary organization, stormed their house, brandishing weapons. Her Tutsi husband was shot and killed. Her toddler son was also brutally murdered. "It's not an easy story to tell," Beatha whispered in the dusky shadows of day's end. "When I think back, I don't think humans did those things. Those were animal acts."

Beatha survived the attack in part because her baby, strapped tightly to her back, met the murderous thrusts of the machetes. For four days Beatha lay lifeless, pretending to be dead and only daring to move when the dogs circled to feed on the corpses. Weakening from thirst and wounded by war, Beatha survived on the spilled blood of her family. She was eventually rescued and reunited with her three surviving children, who had been sent away before the genocide began. But deafened, disabled, and desperately poor, she sank into hopelessness. "I couldn't provide for my children. I couldn't lift myself up," she recounted. "They survived by eating garbage."

Several months later a neighborhood woman told Beatha about the small loans Urwego Opportunity Bank (HOPE's Rwandan partner) was offering to genocide survivors: 15,000 Rwandan francs—*twenty American dollars*. "My friend forced me to take the loan, insisting she would pay it back if I couldn't," Beatha explained. "She said, 'We know you used to be a warrior woman. You are capable.'"

With Urwego's loan and the skills she had gained from previous vocational training, Beatha launched a small business making handcrafts and clothes. "God blessed my hands, even in that condition." After four months she repaid her loan. And took another. And another. Twenty years later, business booms. Beatha lives in a well-kept house with a small yard. She employs a staff. She has sent her children through school. And maybe this is one of the best examples of the feast that God means to bring to earth as it is in heaven—food for the hungry, requiring no linen table-cloth or fancy furniture, only the hopeful generosity of God's people and the willing hands of work.

In 1962, in the segregated southern United States, Fannie Lou Hamer left the cotton fields to work as a civil rights activist. She considered the movement for racial justice like a "welcoming table, the kind that might be found beside a rural Baptist church, where on special Sundays and dinners-on-the-ground, the abundant riches of southern cooking would be spread out for everyone to enjoy—even [segregationist] Governor Ross Barnett and Senator James O. Eastland, though they would need to learn some manners."[13] Hamer knew what Israel knew and what Jesus knew: that a table is central to the kingdom of God, that a feast makes for a home.

In fact, even a cup of cold water offered in the name of Jesus Christ receives its reward.

10

CATHEDRAL IN TIME
A Place Called Rest

408 HOLLY AVENUE
ELMHURST, ILLINOIS

IT WAS THE HOTTEST MAY ON RECORD in Illinois. I was thirty-six weeks pregnant with our third child when we moved into my husband's childhood home. We had just sold our house in Ohio to purchase and begin renovating a house in the western suburbs of Chicago, and for two months we took up temporary residence in the upstairs of the 1920s brick Georgian only recently outfitted with air-conditioning. My mother-in-law and father-in-law invested in a rolling clothing rack and slept on the sleeper sofa in the basement. Camille was born three weeks later, and we brought her "home" from the hospital on Memorial Day. That afternoon, my mother-in-law made me my routine cup of afternoon coffee.

After two months of shared space, our family moved into a rental house, which finally became available in July. The split-level on Huntington Lane was sparsely furnished with the few items we'd confiscated from our storage unit: mattresses and box springs, Ryan's desk, a handful of baby items as well as a borrowed dining table, chairs, and couch. Once Camille began sleeping through the night, we moved her out of our bedroom into a Pack 'n Play among the towers of unpacked boxes in the half-basement, confining her to a dark corner so that Ryan would not disturb her when he stayed up late studying. The house on Huntington Lane was always meant to be an impermanent address, which may have been my reason for never once having used or cleaned the small bathroom in the basement. We lived more lightly there than anywhere in our marriage.

Nearly ever afternoon of that late summer and fall, I made a daily event of monitoring the progress of our house renovations, three blocks away, with the children. The short walk, preoccupied with picking up the porcupine-backed horse chestnuts fallen from the neighbor's tree, consumed part of the interminable stretch between naptime and bedtime, and the percussive concert of nail guns and hammers mesmerized the knee-high audience. It was unlikely that Ryan was coming home from work before heading to graduate school. I was, once again, the lone circus performer, left to tame the animals. There was time to kill.

Life, on the other side of a geographical move, echoes like an empty house, and it is lonely to unpack one's life in another place. Worse, when we arrived in Elmhurst, I seemed simply to have gone from one weariness to another. In the first several months of her life, Camille nursed poorly and gained weight too slowly. Ryan was diagnosed with diabetes. With three children three and younger, the days bled one into another, ringing with noise and spinning like a top. To get out of the house in the morning by myself for weekly Bible study required the foresight and strict execution of emergency preparedness: the night before, clothes and breakfasts were readied and the diaper bag was packed (and packed in the car). Every day struck with tsunami force, and only by running full speed did I think I could outwit the daily violence. But I was good at running, good at keeping my eye on the clock.

But to run is eventually to run out of breath. Soon I realized that life was not ever going to slow for me—that I would have to slow for it. Slowing, in fact, would be my only hope of living life, not simply surviving it. And so, in one of the most improbable seasons of my life, I started practicing sabbath, nudged toward the discipline of rest by Gordon MacDonald's book *Ordering Your Private World.* "If my private world is in order," writes MacDonald, "it will be because I have chosen to press Sabbath peace into the rush and routine of my daily life in order to find the rest God prescribed for himself and all of humanity."[1] As the mother of three young children, I gave up, for one day of the week, the rush to get ahead. The alternative felt like death.

OUR LONGING FOR REST

If sabbath seems tangential to the topic of home, which implies geography of place more than architecture of time, it's interesting to note that the visible evidence of God's rest in Genesis 2 isn't his sleeping but his place of residence. On the seventh day God is enthroned in his creation. As he takes leave from his labor, he rests.

Rest is, of course, one image used in the Scriptures to describe the eternal inheritance of the people of God—their *home.* As the people of Israel learned, the Promised Land was a place of rest. Nevertheless, as the writer of Hebrews explains, if Moses' successor, Joshua, led the people of Israel into the land of Canaan and provided military leadership for their campaign of war, he

never provided the rest God's people had anticipated. According
to Hebrews, there remains a greater rest for the people of God,
a "sabbath rest," which we must all strive to enter by avoiding
the pitfalls of unbelief and disobedience. Like the Israelites entered Canaan, where they were sheltered by God's provision and
protection, there is a rest awaiting us where we will lay down our
toil and cease from our labor.

Rest is contrapuntal to the call to keep house.

"At some point, we all look for a Sabbath, whether or not
that's what we call it," writes Judith Shulevitz in the opening of
her book *The Sabbath World: Glimpses of a Different Order of Time.*
As a young Jewish girl, Shulevitz had not been raised to strictly
observe the sabbath, although she did return, in later adulthood,
to a piqued interest in sabbath observance. "At the core of the
Sabbath," she writes, "lives an unassuageable longing."[2] We long
for, as Rabbi Abraham Joshua Heschel has called it, a cathedral
of time in our week: a day set apart, consecrated, made holy by
its otherness.

Shulevitz explains the rabbinic tradition regarding the seventh
day of rest, given by God to his people.

> The Sabbath, said the rabbis, is a bride given by God to her
> groom, the people of Israel. Once a week, they go forth in
> wedding clothes to marry her. The Sabbath, said the rabbis,
> is a gift from God's treasury. Once a week, his people re-
> ceive it and are enriched. The Sabbath, said the rabbis, is
> the Temple in time rather than space. Once a week, every
> Jew becomes a priest and enters it. The Sabbath, said the
> rabbis, is the Chosen Day, just as the children of Israel are
> the Chosen People.[3]

Despite the onerous restrictions regarding the thirty-nine cate-
gories of work forbidden from the setting of the sun on Friday

to its setting on Saturday (more than 250 two-sided pages are dedicated to *Shabbat* boundaries in the Talmudic tractate), the Sabbath, as the Jews understand it, is a holy day sanctified for joy. It is a day given by God for the rejoicing of his people.

There is joy in regular, rhythmic reprieve from the weary world of work for both the Jew and Gentile—even if work was initially given to God's people as blessing, not curse. After the fall, however, humanity's work of tilling the ground and multiplying their off-spring turned to toil, and since that time, work has had an inhuman capacity for reducing us to mere machinery. Work holds the reins, drives us forward faster. This is no truer than in modern economics, where human beings are worth no more than their labor, their hours, no more than their productive output.

Sabbath, as understood by ancient Jews, laid claim to human-ity's dignity as much as it laid claim to humanity's time. A day of rest was an act of resistance in exactly the way that Pharaoh understood Moses' request for three-day leave from brick making for the purposes of keeping festival to Israel's God. "Why do you take the people away from their work?" Pharaoh demanded. "Get back to your burdens" (Ex 5:4). Then and now, in ancient Egypt as in Manhattan, the leisure of sabbath threatens the ex-acting demands of the daily quota. It requires courage of all who would take it up.

Based on recent book publishing history, Shulevitz claims that there is a resurgence of interest in the sabbath today, albeit sabbath less as a religious practice and more as a habit of self-improvement. We are wrung out by the 24/7 demands of today's mobile work environment and hungry for a small slice of stillness and quiet. We want to recover what boundaryless work has stolen from our evenings and weekends, from our families and inner quietude. We want to reclaim ourselves from the inhumanity of work without pause, that "bare, hopeless effort [that] resembles the labor of Sisyphus, who in fact is the mythical paradigm of the 'Worker' chained to his labor without rest, and without inner satisfaction."[4] We want to unearth what's meaningful about life apart from labor and measure our worth by something other than the almighty dollar. At the end of the week, we are spent and sabbath-hungry.

We want to rest. Which is to say, we want to go home.

THE OLD TESTAMENT PRACTICE OF SABBATH

The first mention of the sabbath is not, as we might expect, the fourth commandment of Moses' Ten Words, given on Mount Sinai to legislate the social, civil, and ceremonial life of the new nation of Israel. Instead, the first sabbath appears before it has ever been codified into law—when the first manna falls, like dew, from heaven.

The Israelites have left behind Egypt more than a month earlier, and their provisions, which they had hastily packed for the journey, have run out. Despite that God has just miraculously provided water for the thirsty multitude, they mistrust his willingness to provide food, pining instead for the Egyptian fare they had left behind. "Would that we had died by the hand of the LORD in the land of Egypt, when we sat by the meat pots and ate bread to the full" (Ex 16:3). Four times the text makes explicit mention of their collective complaint, described as grumbling before the Lord. They shake their fists at the heavens and accuse Moses of murderous intent.

That the God of Israel is a patient God, slow to anger and abounding in steadfast love, is no more evident than in his unwillingness to let his people starve. Rather than punishing them for their unbelief, he makes manifest his glory in the form of a blanket of quail in the evening and a dusting of bread in the morning. He gives them manna, and he gives them mercy. You shall know that I am the Lord your God when I feed you, he tells them, and his people wake to a strange, "flake-like thing" comparable to winter frost, which he commands to be gathered six days of the week. None must be stored, else it become rancid. On the seventh day they are instructed to stay home because it is a "day of solemn rest, a holy Sabbath to the Lord" (v. 23). At first, of course, they heed none of these instructions, failing the test God has given to determine "whether they will walk in my law or not" (v. 4). They try storing manna overnight, and they wake on the seventh day, as on the previous six, foraging for food. The people of Israel, like us, were not easily weaned from their anxieties and habits of self-reliance.

In the first sabbath story, we see the seventh day of rest as yet another extravagant expression of God's goodness and grace toward his undeserving people. The manna isn't the only gift falling from heaven. As verse 29 says, the Lord also gave the gift of the sabbath. Though the people of Israel might have been contented to rise seven mornings at dawn, leaving their tents to gather the manna before the sun grew hot overhead, God obligated them to a day of rest. He forbade their labor and created space for their leisure. And though they wouldn't gather the manna on the seventh day, they would still eat, for the manna gathered on the sixth day would provide sufficient supply for the sabbath, a lesson that food security depended not on their gathering but on God's providing.

Throughout the sabbath story of Exodus 16, the act of gathering seems almost incidental to supply. When someone gathered little, it was always ample provision. When someone gathered much, nothing was wasted. The text even seems to invite speculation as to what really happened in the fields and kitchens on day six: in the pre-dawn hours of Friday, did the people gather two omers rather than one? Or did they watch the manna multiply as they kneaded the bread and watched it bake? (Verse 5 states, *"When they prepare* what they bring in, it will be twice as much as they gather daily."*) Either way, on the seventh day, God satisfied the hunger of his people, fulfilling an obvious bodily need. But in addition to physical sustenance, God also granted his people a gift they hadn't thought to desire, a gift they might even have willingly refused if it hadn't been forced upon them.

It was the provision of rest.

In Exodus 20, sabbath observance is given as a command to the people of God. Strikingly, however, the Israelites are not commanded to "practice" the sabbath but "remember" it, as if sabbath were lines of a dramatic play weekly rehearsed. Saturday wasn't simply a day obediently consecrated to rest. It was a covenantal liturgy for the people of God given for cultivating holy memory. The story of sabbath began, of course, long before Exodus 16 and the gift of the manna. It began with the rest God took after his six days of laboring over the world. Though the God of Spirit had no need to rest his weary bones, he paused from his labor and reveled in the very good world he had made. He declared rest very good by his own embrace of pause.

We regularly rest because we are made in the image of a working and resting God. To remember the sabbath is to remember the full stop that God put to his own work, a God who is never anxious or hurried. His rest signaled, as John Walton writes in *The Lost World of Genesis One*, his confident command of the planets he had spun into orbit, the animals he had commanded to teem, the human beings he had expired breath into and appointed as co-regents of the earth. Humanity's home was in order: all was right with the world. And so God rested. We rest, remembering that the world coheres at his command—and that home has never depended on our housekeeping. To be sure, God's kingdom is at hand, and the people of God must be about his business. Nevertheless, the sabbath reminds us that at the end of every day and week, it remains, fully and finally, *his* business.

If the people of Israel were meant to remember God's rest on the sabbath day, they were also to remember Egypt and their former slavery (Deut 5:15). As we've already seen from Exodus 16, the people of Israel frequently misremembered their history of oppression. When they hungered in the wilderness, they re-membered Egypt as meat pots and bread loaves, failing to recall the bricks and the blows of their taskmasters. They forgot their groaning, their desperate hope for rescue, and their own cries for help that rose to God when they provided the slave labor for Egyptian construction projects. But if they forgot, God remem-bered: "And God heard their groaning, and God remembered his covenant with Abraham, with Isaac, and with Jacob" (Ex 2:24). God had intervened in their desperation and freed them because he, unlike they, would not forget or fail a promise. To remember the sabbath is to remember God's remembering.

The sabbath, like each of the Ten Words, was a commandment to love God and to love neighbor. As the Exodus 20 text makes clear, sabbath keeping wasn't simply a private devotional practice enabling a day of quiet contemplation and play. It meted out justice for all laborers, allowing them, as well as the land, to rest. Sabbath prescribed fallowness. Indeed, God had warned Israel about failing to observe sabbath, which would abuse the land. In the (sure) event of their rebellion, he would make their overwork unproductive and exile them from the land. "The land shall enjoy its Sabbaths," God declared prophetically in Leviticus 26:34. When I drive you from your home, I will give the fields and valleys and rivers the rest you refused them.

Remember the sabbath and keep it holy, God says. Sabbath tells a different story. It makes each of us a different character in the drama. "There is perhaps no single thing that could better help us recover Jesus' lordship in our frantic, power-hungry world," writes Andy Crouch in *Playing God*, "than to allow him to be Lord of our rest as well as our work. The challenge is disarmingly simple: one day a week, not to do anything that we know to be work."[5]

A CHRISTIAN SABBATH

For Christians, strict sabbath observance is not axiomatic to our faith. It wasn't until the second century, in fact, that Sunday became the standard day for Christian worship, and even then, followers of Jesus did not quit work on Sundays. Most early Christians, in fact, were poorer members of society without the privilege of seventh-day rest, and they would have assembled for worship early in the morning before punching the clock. Not until AD 321 was sabbath observance codified in civic law, when Constantine, the newly Christianized emperor, banned official business and manufacturing on Sunday.

Throughout the course of human history Christians have disagreed about their obligation to remember the sabbath and keep it holy. At the time of the Reformation, Martin Luther taught the necessity of sabbath observance but shied from insisting on prescriptive rules. John Calvin disagreed with Luther that the sabbath was binding on Christians (as it had been on Jews), but he did affirm its social good "insofar as it promoted communal worship, and general piety, and gave servants a rest."[6]

Historically, the group of people most zealous for the sabbath and most familiar to North American readers might have been the Puritans: "They had such a deep hunger for the Sabbath—for the right *kind* of Sabbath—that they left England, whose Sabbaths they considered corrupt and lax, and sailed to America, in order to keep the kind of disciplined, godly Sabbaths they believed would transform their earthly existence into a New Jerusalem."[7] Sabbath, as a spiritual practice, was regarded by the

Puritans as the highest form of housekeeping. It was a way of remaking the world and fitting it to look like heaven.

According to certain historians, the Puritans had a dour view of sabbath, forbidding not simply work but various forms of leisure. "No work, no play, no idle strolling was known," wrote Alice Morse Earle in the nineteenth-century, describing the Puritan sabbath. "No sign of human life or motion was seen except the necessary care of patient cattle and other dumb beasts, the orderly and quiet going to and from the meeting, and at the morning, a visit to the churchyard to stand by the side of the silent dead."[8] Sabbath, for the Puritans, was an extended day for church attendance. The village meeting house opened at 9 a.m. for the first of two services interrupted by lunch. But this was not a day characterized by feasting and gaiety, but rather sobriety and study. Attentiveness was strictly enforced during services by threat of corporal punishment. "Should a churchgoer nod off to sleep, he might be woken by a tithing man, a member of the congregation appointed to wander the building with a long staff. The staff had a knob on one end and a foxtail hanging from the other, and the tithing man would either rap the sleeper on the head or slap the fur against her face until she woke up."[9] The Puritans did not endure half-hearted, sleepy sabbath keepers.

Jesus was certainly less strict than the Puritans and the Pharisees of his day in keeping the sabbath holy. Saturday laxity was leveled as a frequent charge against him. Though it was Jesus' custom to worship regularly at the synagogue on Saturday, throughout the Gospel of Luke, Jesus is often perceived to be "working" on the sabbath: he and his disciples pluck heads of grain, rubbing them in their hands; he heals a man with a withered hand; he helps a woman stand straight after eighteen years of crippling disability; he heals a man with a severe case of edema. For these perceived "lapses" in sabbath keeping, Jesus is called a lawbreaker.

What did and did not constitute "lawful" activity on the sabbath was cause for frequent dispute between Jesus and the religious leaders of his day. "There are six days in which work ought to be done," the ruler of one synagogue announced on Saturday to the crowds seeking Jesus for reprieve from their physical disabilities. "Come on those days and be healed, and not on the Sabbath day," he chided (Lk 13:14). But Jesus frequently contends that the lawfulness of certain activities on the sabbath can be defended by the extent to which they accomplish good. "It is lawful to do good on the Sabbath," he concluded, defending his healings and demon deliverances as well as reminding the Pharisees of their frequent hypocrisy. "Does not each of you on the Sabbath untie his ox or his donkey from the manger and lead it away to water it?" (Lk 13:15). "Which of you, having a son or an ox that has fallen into a well on a Sabbath day, will not immediately pull him out?" (Lk 14:5).

Claiming God as his Father—the God who, after the seventh day of creation, ceaselessly continues the work of sustaining the world—Jesus defended his sabbath activities. But this blasphemous assertion of divinity, rather than acquitting him, enrages the religious leaders even further. No sabbath breaker could be the rightful Son of God. As N. T. Wright asserts, "Loyal Jews of the last few centuries BC made Sabbath-keeping one of the major distinctive marks [of being a Jew], to the point where one of the few things the average pagan knew about the strange Jewish people living in their midst (along with circumcision and the food taboos) was that they had a lazy day once a week."[10] Sabbath observance in the first century wasn't a secondary requirement of faithfulness. It was primary.

Unlike his critics accused, Jesus did not disparage the sabbath in particular or the Mosaic law in general. Rather, he saw himself as the fulfillment of the Law and the Prophets—the reality to which all the signs, including the sabbath, had pointed. "Come to me," Jesus called to the weary. "I will give you rest. Take my yoke upon you, and learn from me, for I am gentle and lowly in heart, and you will find rest for your souls. For my yoke is easy, and my burden is light" (Mt 11:28-30). As Paul put it in Romans 2:16, the sabbath was the "shadow" while the substance was Christ.

N. T. Wright explains that the bodily resurrection of Jesus of Nazareth announced the dawning of a new creation. To insist on the old order of things, including the total forbiddance of work on the sabbath, was "like someone insisting on continuing to plough the field at the very moment when the crop was beginning to come up."[11] If Jesus is the eternal sabbath, to be united with him is to rest—not one day, but seven.

151 GLENDON AVENUE
TORONTO, ONTARIO

At the beginning of a new year, I decide to rest. I finally decide because no one will decide for me, no matter how much I wish for the collective permission to excuse myself, if momentarily, from the burdens of my housekeeping. I will catch my breath as God caught his, according to Exodus 31:17.[12] I will be still and know that he is God—or, as Josef Pieper put it in his essay "Leisure: The Basis of Culture," I will be *at leisure* and know that God is God. For a month I will commit to learning that not everything can be gained or learned from hard work. I will be apprenticed by rest.

When Pieper wrote his essay, the Second World War had just ended, and he anticipated objections to his defense of leisure. Some will say, "We are engaged in the re-building of the house, and our hands are full."[13] Surely no one could be implored to rest when there was so much political, social, and economic work to be done in the world as the Holocaust fires turned to ash and communism flared up as the next unholy blaze. But Pieper insisted on the idea of rest, which he defended as the scaffolding of "our entire moral and intellectual heritage."[14] Work, he writes, can only make sense when it is informed by leisure—or better yet, *worship*, which is the leisurely work of receiving the world and celebrating its Maker. "Leisure is a form of stillness that is necessary preparation for accepting reality; only the person who is still can hear, and whoever is not still, cannot hear. Such stillness as this is not mere soundlessness or a dead muteness. . . . Leisure is a disposition of receptive understanding, of contemplative beholding, and immersion—in the real."[15] According to Pieper, there is necessary stillness and worshipful silence in rest.

For the moment of a month, I entered a new year with rest at the top of my to-dos. I didn't hustle the kids back to school. I didn't make ambitious resolutions. I turned down writing assignments and took up poetry. Bid by the quiet voice of God, I let go of the reins of life and stopped driving so mercilessly hard. Can it be any wonder that the full stop was grace-full? We are not beasts of burden: we are made of flesh, and God has compassion on the limitations of our bodies. "For he knows our frame; / he remembers that we are dust" (Ps 103:14). To practice sabbath as a commitment to regular rest is to let God love us apart from our efforts and contribution, and it's the housekeeping of rest that enables us to value the humanity in others.

Protracted rest forced me to confront some of my own disordered desires. On the one hand, I wished to be free from burdens of the housekeeping. Truthfully, I wanted people to stop bothering me. I didn't want to have to answer email or make dinner, finish the laundry or return a friend's phone call. Plagued with my own strand of acedia, I wanted to plump the proverbial pillows and protect my hard work from being ruined by another person's carelessness. I greedily craved the still life, which Luci Shaw paints in her poem:

I'd like to arrange
A still life
And then
Go live in it—
An artful pot,
Dried flowers,
A stone frog
Whose eyes
Never blink,
And perfect calm.[16]

But as Shaw so trenchantly illustrates, a still life is a dead life. Housekeeping, however onerous, is evidence of breath.

If I wanted to be rid of the housekeeping, I also too desperately needed it. I wished to be told that my contribution was urgent, invaluable, brilliant. I cherished, however much I also hated, the illusion of being inextricable. Work, without rest, had been one way of assuring myself that I mattered in the world. Little wonder that the prophet Isaiah said that salvation would be found "in returning and rest" (Is 30:15). Maybe it is rest that makes a different kind of returning home—or "repentance"— possible. Maybe it's why God calls home "rest."

In the second half of this book I have argued for the importance of the housekeeping. The kingdom of God has never relied on life-changing magic. Instead, it commissions hands and feet—a cohort of servants who declare with the prophet Isaiah, *I'm here! Send me!* It is impossible to love the world apart from labor, and the gospel story of home inspires housework. "For the grace of God has appeared . . . [and our] Savior Christ . . . gave himself . . . to purify a people for his own possession who are zealous for good works" (Titus 2:11-14).

But our labor is never the first or final word, even if, in a very real sense, we will still be about the sacred tasks of housekeeping on the new earth. There is a God who works on humanity's behalf. He is the Homemaker who keeps his people, and he will neither slumber nor sleep (Ps 121:3-4). The Lord is always about the housekeeping: in our families, in our churches, in our cities, and in the world. This doesn't relieve us of our responsibilities to humbly share in his burdens of mercy and justice, but it does permit us to rest, practicing sabbath as protection from the clamor of our own desires and our megalomania. We do not have the whole world in our hands.

A decision to rest is as much for Monday as for Sundays. It is a humble nod to the limits of our bodies and time. It is a plea of vulnerability; it is a cry of dependence. But it is not simply a practice to *restore* us, as if we idled our bodies only to improve their performance. Rather, sabbath is a practice to *re-story* us. To remind us of the God who feeds, the God who rescues, the God who himself rests.

> Let *your work* be shown to your servants,
>   and your glorious power to their children.
> Let the favor of the Lord our God be upon us,
>   and establish the work of our hands upon us;
>   yes, establish the work of our hands. (Ps 90:16-17)

Pause is a practice of remembering the Creator and his work while acknowledging our creatureliness. Maybe in this way, it is, as the Puritans called it, a necessary form of housekeeping, even if it is simultaneously abandonment of it.

We return home and rest—and know that he is God.

11

CITY OF GOD
Finally Home

3213 TUTTLE PLACE, APARTMENT 3B
DUBLIN, OHIO

I LEAVE FOR TORONTO EARLIER THAN PLANNED, even
if it means having to pass the Cleveland Chick-fil-A where I've
hoped to buy lunch. I trust my mother to the doubtful care of
her husband, twelve years her senior, and kiss them both at the
door. As one last gesture of the housekeeping, I heave the
kitchen trash into the large dumpster of their apartment
complex. When my stepfather, Don, offers to help me with my
suitcase, I refuse out of necessity. Age is stealing his capacity for
small kindnesses.

"It's hard to be old," he rues each morning of my weeklong
visit. I watch him struggle to shimmy socks up his legs. His
fingers tremble with Parkinson's and prevent him from buttoning

his own shirt. "Jan?" he calls from the bedroom, helpless to pull a knit sweater over his head. My mother shuffles from the kitchen and offers help with her left arm, her right arm dangling at her side because of the recent mastectomy—her second in eight years. Just four weeks earlier, she learned that cancer had returned to finish the job.

At the time of her first diagnosis, I was thirty-four weeks pregnant with twin boys, living in Illinois while she lived in Ohio. And though I tried to absorb the news, the urgent daily demands of children replaced the duties I might have responsibly upheld during the months of her treatment. I failed to write or call often. But when chemotherapy thinned her hair to tumbleweed, I was the one to razor her head. Her hair fell in clumps at my feet, and as the first to see her baldness, I hope that counts for something.

In the wake of my mom's most recent surgery, I traveled to Ohio to take up her housekeeping. I vacuumed. I rolled meatballs. I replaced the broken toaster. Every morning and every afternoon, I brewed a batch of strong coffee and sat smiling around the table, answering questions I might have already answered tens of times. I spent the week with my mother and stepfather because I wanted to help. Or, better yet, I wanted *to want* to help. Surely that must mean that by God's grace, years of accumulated resentment are thawing, and forgiveness is cobbling a footpath. I take it home.

Twenty years after Gordon Crosby moved to Washington, DC, in the late 1940s to start Church of the Savior, as a result of the church's obvious success, Crosby began to be invited to speak across the country. As Jonathan Wilson-Hartgrove details in *The Wisdom of Stability*, Cosby initially accepted as many of these engagements as he could, reasoning that the public exposure could extend the reach of his church's ministry. But he soon discovered how difficult it was to keep up the difficult work of pastoring while frequently traveling. Eventually, Cosby heard God speak to him in an undeniable way. "The message was simple: 'Stay home and do your knitting.'"[1]

Home and its housekeeping is a call to the knitting. God's work is not nearly as glamorous as our self-glorifying ambitions. In fact, it is as unassuming and quietly aspiring as the commitment to forgive and to help. Perhaps this is what Benedictine monks learned from inside the monastery walls. When they pledged to stay put, they also promised to embrace "a particular community, this place and these people, this and no other, as the way to God."[2] Their stability was an obedient commitment to whatever was daily and whomever was closest; in devotion to God, they kept up the practice of embodied, localized love.

Stability, as commitment to place, and enclosure, as commitment to people, aim to prove that demons are not easily left behind. Home, on this earth, is no perfect place, and one of our greatest acts of faithful courage might be abiding the weariness of imperfect company, both that of ourselves and others. As Edith Schaeffer writes in her book *What Is a Family?*, "When people insist on perfection or nothing, they get nothing. When people insist on having what they daydream as a perfect relationship, they will end up having no relationship at all."[3] Housekeeping is home's daily chore of faith, hope, and love. It doesn't hold out for what might never be. Instead, it wrings good from what is.

MADE FOR ANOTHER WORLD

Nearly fifteen years ago my brother-in-law and sister-in-law moved into the neighborhood of Lawndale, a predominantly African American community on Chicago's West Side. Hope can seem as vacant as many of the lots. Billy Brooks, who was

raised in Lawndale and continues to work in the neighborhood, describes the implicit messages kids growing up in
Lawndale receive: "You ain't sh——. You no good. The only
thing you are worth is working for us. You will never own
anything. You not going to get an education. We are sending
your a—— to the penitentiary."[4]

In the middle of the Great Migration, when millions of blacks
were escaping the South to find better lives in the North,
Lawndale was the stage for corrupt, racist real estate practices.
Today, it struggles to recover from that legacy of injustice.
"Chicago is one of the most segregated cities in the United States,
a fact that reflects assiduous planning," writes Ta-Nehisi Coates
in his cover article for *The Atlantic.* In 1917 the Chicago Real
Estate Board lobbied to zone the entire city by race, and while
this explicit attempt to segregate blacks and whites was struck
down by a Supreme Court ruling, Chicago pursued other ne-
farious policies. When Chicago built their public housing units
in the middle of the century, they put them in all-black neighborhoods. The city prevented blacks from receiving federally
backed home loans, which might have allowed them to move
into more prosperous (white) neighborhoods. In neighborhoods
such as Lawndale, whites began fleeing for the suburbs as a result
of scare tactics. "With these white-fled homes in hand . . . spec-
ulators would take the houses they'd just bought cheap through
block-busting and sell them to blacks on contract."[5]

These "on contract" real estate agreements were ruthlessly
predatory. If the new homeowner missed a single payment, he
forfeited his house and all the money invested in it. Once this
family was evicted, "[the peddlers would] bring in another black
family, rinse, and repeat."[6]

My brother- and sister-in-law and their three children have
vowed stability to Lawndale and its people, and the relationships

they have built over fences and around kitchen tables have provided inroads of participation in their neighborhood's common good, including a community garden, an educational scholarship fund for local children, afterschool tutoring clubs, and summer Vacation Bible School. Their patience of staying put is paying off for Christ and his kingdom, and I can't help but envy their rootedness and its clear reward.

If Lawndale seems like a particularly destitute version of home, neither will lakefront property on Chicago's North Shore satisfy our longing for home. Wherever we find ourselves, our earthly homes fail all of us. "The houses and families we actually inhabit," writes Tim Keller, "are only inns along the way, but they aren't home."[7] Death, divorce, unexpected illness, and financial uncertainty: like claps of thunder, these portend that humanity huddles together under a cauldron sky, readied to tip and pour out suffering. Home isn't always refuge. We pine for marriage and stay single. We want children and birth barrenness. At our tables too many of us find loneliness instead of company. And immune though we may be in North America from the domestic ravages of war and famine, we watch as home's broken promises wash up on beaches facedown. None of us, not even those of us in middle-class America, can be persuaded that this is the best of all possible worlds. Home, as we presently inhabit it, is not the dream we dreamed, and all of us suffer from what C. S. Lewis describes as a "life-long nostalgia, [a] longing to be reunited with something in the universe from which we feel cut off, to be on the inside of some door which we have always seen from the outside."[8] Displacement is our low-grade fever.

It hurts to be hard from home. But perhaps our common grief—of crossing borders, mourning death, lamenting strained relationships, and generally feeling earth's ill-fit—is a severe mercy. No doubt it helps us understand that home is not now, not yet. Homelessness teaches us, not least, that something has gone terribly wrong in the world.

On Saturday, December 4, 2015, in the wake of the terrorist gun spree in San Bernardino, California, which killed fourteen and wounded twenty-one, the *New York Times* ran its first front-page editorial since 1920, opening with lamentation at a world gone wrong. "All decent people feel sorrow and righteous fury about the lastest slaughter of innocents in California," the piece begins. When human light can be so violently put out, when safety becomes our naiveté, the world is not home.[9]

Only one plausible explanation remains for the consensus that the home has been ransacked: a good world has gone terribly wrong. That is the story as the Christian gospel tells it. When the world began, according to the Scriptures, it was *very good*: good for humanity, for whose survival everything was particularly suited, and good for God, who took his rest and enthroned himself in the temple of his creation. In the beginning we rightfully recognized him as Lord of the house. Nevertheless, preferring self-rule to submission, we transgressed the house rules, and God suffered our leave-taking. The very good world, subjected to cosmic vandalism, now groans with its own longing for redemption (Rom 8:18-22). As God's people, we bear witness to the reasons for humanity's lament. Things are going to hurt in this present life; it's one symptom of mutability.

Our desire for home is presently unrequited despite our many and varied ways of trying to console our grief. We cannot buy our way to home or move to find it. And in the face of that disappointment, C. S. Lewis suggests we have three choices. First, we can "put the blame on the things themselves."[10] This is the Fool's Way, says Lewis, and it is taken by those who "spend their whole lives trotting from woman to woman (through the divorce courts), from continent to continent, from hobby to hobby, always thinking that the latest is 'the Real Thing' at last, and always disappointed."[11] The fool looks for a new home when his present one fails him. As an alternative to this foolishness, we can choose to repress our desires. This is the "Way of the Disillusioned 'Sensible Man,'" who, according to Lewis, no longer cries for the moon (or home). He resigns himself to a fateful dose of realism, which might be admirable except, "Supposing infinite happiness really is there, waiting for us? Supposing one really can reach rainbow's end?"[12] The third way, writes Lewis, is the Christian way, and it is not taken by those who seek to ultimately satisfy their desires in this world, nor is it taken by those who would abandon desiring altogether. Instead, the Christian is the one who rightly appraises the function of desire: "The Christian says, 'Creatures are not born with desires unless satisfaction for those desires exists. . . . [But] if I find in myself a desire which no experience in this world can satisfy, the most probable explanation is that I was made for another world.'"[13] The desire for home is a good desire, and the Bible assures us that if we want home, we shall have it. Just not in this life.

WILLINGNESS TO WAIT

The longing for home is associated with memory: a paradise was in fact lost. It also looks ahead, inspiring our hope for inhabiting the eternal City of God. Redeemed humanity has a keeping place. Some readers might wish that I had been more specific about the nature of the new heavens and the new earth, but the truth is I have not settled my own curiosities, and better books have been written on the subject.[14] Like N. T. Wright, I can't help but recognize that "all language about the future, as any economist or politician will tell you, is simply a set of signposts pointing into a fog. We see through a glass darkly, says St. Paul as he peers towards what lies ahead."[15] For as certain as I am about my future home with God, I feel like the bride wearing a blindfold and awaiting her surprise. I don't know what to expect aside from knowing that it will be beyond my asking or imagining.

As many Christian writers and thinkers have argued, it is upon our longings for eternity that the whole of Christian life depends. We must become the kind of people who learn to look ahead and yearn for all that's promised beyond death. This isn't, of course, to say that we despise the present world. As C. S. Lewis has claimed, "If you read history you will find that the Christians who did more for the present world were just those who thought most of the next. The Apostles themselves, who set on foot the conversion of the Roman Empire, the great men who built up the Middle Ages, the English Evangelicals who abolished the Slave Trade, all left their mark on Earth, precisely because their minds were occupied with heaven."[16] Eternal hope of the biblical kind does not inspire selfish indifference to earthly suffering. It informs a redemptive vision of an earth where God's will is done as it is in heaven. Without a view of the new heavens and the new earth, we fail the housekeeping.

We need to keep the new Jerusalem in our sights lest we become the proverbial child who fails the Stanford marshmallow experiment. When offered one marshmallow now or two marshmallows in fifteen minutes, we will be tempted to gobble the present treat rather than wait for the better reward.[17] The wisdom of home begs witness and work as much as hope and holiness. If the universe is divested of lights, as Camus has insisted, if God is dead and home a fairytale fiction, then let us "eat and drink, for tomorrow we die" (1 Cor 15:32). But if eternity does stretch beyond the horizon of life, if there is a home, a Homemaker, and a generous invitation to the feast, let us "abide in him so that when he appears, we may have confidence and not shrink from him in shame at his coming" (1 Jn 2:28).

When our family crossed the Canadian border this past Christmas, we were required to process our temporary work visas in person with immigration officials. As we expected, there was no visible hurry on the part of border control officers to do so, and our family, having already spent six hours in the car, waited another three hours in the lobby. Though I hadn't been optimistic about the day's timeline, neither had I exercised the foresight to pack sufficient supplies for five tired, hungry, and stir-crazy children. We suffered that wait more than necessary. But perhaps what kept us all going was the knowledge that the wait was going to produce something good, something our family had been praying for: a piece of paper extending our permission to stay in Canada.

Home helps us outlast our sufferings. We can admit our disappointments, grieve our losses, but recognize, with stubborn joy, that they are *temporary*. When seasons of unwanted singleness or infertility persist, when our marriages end, when a child dies, when the doctor delivers an unwanted diagnosis, we remember this earth is the lineup to the real event, and grief is one sure symptom of exile.

THE FAR COUNTRY

If home is to be so inexorably desired, home can be found. But if home, in this life, should fail to deliver, we must learn to look for it elsewhere. It's no use, of course, saying that we shouldn't be hungry. A keen appetite is, in fact, necessary for the feast, and there are smells wafting from the kitchen. But neither should we spoil our dinner with empty calories, which fail to satisfy. The longing for home is "the scent of a flower we have not found, the echo of a tune we have not heard, news from a country we have never yet visited."[18] It signals that one day, the Son will rise to end creation's longest night:

To an open house in the evening
Home shall men come,
To an older place than Eden
And a taller town than Rome.
To the end of the way of the wandering star,
To the things that cannot be and that are,
To the place where God was homeless
And all men are at home.[19]

To God's great chagrin, however, not all are welcomed home—and not all wish to be. And this is Lewis's trenchant point of *The Great Divorce*: "All that are in Hell, choose it. Without that self-choice there could be no Hell. No soul that seriously and constantly desires joy will ever miss it. Those who seek find. To those who knock it is opened."[20] God will not force family upon the rebellious son, home upon the willful wanderer. If we want the far country, as did the younger brother in the parable of the prodigal son, to our great grief, we shall have it.

We cannot talk about home as it exists gloriously in the new heavens and the new earth without broaching the subject of final judgment and speaking of what the Bible makes plain: the wrath of God. Though I, like many, am trained to think of God's patience and benevolence in terms of his willingness to dole out gifts rather than mete out judgment, both will be necessary if home will be *home*. As N. T. Wright discusses in *Surprised by Hope*, God's judgment in the Old Testament was always cause for joy. It meant that the oppressor would be held to account, that the poor and the weak would be delivered. It assured that justice would finally be done. And when it was, all of creation would applaud the God of vindicating might:

Let the heavens be glad, and let the earth rejoice;
    let the sea roar, and all that fills it;

> let the field exult, and everything in it!
> Then shall all the trees of the forest sing for joy
>   before the LORD, for he comes,
>   for he comes to judge the earth.
> He will judge the world in righteousness,
>   and the peoples in his faithfulness. (Ps 96:11-13)

The wicked shudder to consider God's judgment. The righteous rejoice.[21]

Several years ago our family extended friendship to an older man with a long, sordid history. Having suffered severe emotional and sexual abuse as a child, the man learned to numb the pain through addiction, which he funded by crime. For many years this man shuttled in and out of prison before he found his way into our lives. Our family began inviting him, more and more regularly, into our home. We understood the power of Christian hospitality to tangibly express the love of Jesus, and we believed that by God's renewing, inhabiting Spirit, this man could be granted the power to change. He needed a home, and we had one to share.

And then he attempted to prey on one of our children, a scandal that exploded on Christmas Eve. As soon as we learned of his intention—thwarted, by God's mercy before harm was done—we confronted him directly, presenting facts, which he duly denied. We were angry and demanded an accounting of his actions, but to this day, despite ample evidence to the contrary, this man maintains his innocence. And though it has broken our heart, on the counsel of several pastors and trained mental-health professionals, we have withdrawn from him our welcome. I am pained to admit, borrowing language from Miroslav Volf, that our home has necessarily become exclusion as well as embrace.

In order for God to be absolutely good to all of his children, then he must judge the misdeeds, even the misdoers.

> Faced with the Balkans, Rwanda, the Middle East, Darfur, and all kinds of other horrors that enlightened Western thought can neither explain nor alleviate, opinion in many quarters has, rightly in my view, come to see that there must be such a thing as judgment. Judgment—the sovereign declaration that *this* is good and to be upheld and vindicated, and *that* is evil and to be condemned—is the only alternative to chaos.[22]

Judgment is necessary for justice to be done in the world, and justice must be done if this world, redeemed and renewed, is to be home. God cannot be good if he is not just. In this way, God's goodness is, as Lewis has aptly said, either the great safety or the great danger.

Judgment is not set aside in God's economy, but neither does it have the last word. According to the Christian gospel, every sinner can flee to the cross of Christ. There, an innocent man was judged in the stead of the guilty, and God's wrath was poured out on his beloved Son. On the cross God made embrace possible rather than exclusion. When we declare faith in Jesus' death and resurrection and anticipate his return, when we admit guilt and renounce self-righteousness, we go free.

Because of the cross, wanderers get home.

HAIL, KING OF THE JEWS

As James Wood recalls in his essay "On Not Going Home," the Greek historian Herodotus credited the military invulnerability of the Scythians to their effective homelessness. They did not live in settled forts or cities. Rather, "they carry their houses with them and shoot with bows from horseback . . . their dwellings are on their wagons. How then can they fail to be invincible and inaccessible for others?" Wood concludes, "To have a home is to become vulnerable. Not just to the attacks of others, but to our own adventures in alienation."[23]

Wood's phrase—"adventure in alienation"—aptly describes the climatic act of the Holy Scriptures: the Incarnation. God entered exile to make possible humanity's homecoming. Jesus *of Nazareth* took up refugee status and entered a world pocked with grief. That all was not right in Jesus' world, as in ours, is evident in each of the Gospel narratives, especially the biographical accounts of Matthew and Luke, which are the only two to situate Jesus' birth during the reign of Herod the Great. Herod (37–4 BC), purported king of the Jews, tried to legitimate his rule by marrying Mariamne, a Hasmonean princess (whose ancestor Judas Maccabaeus had led a guerrilla revolt against Syrian ruler Antiochus Epiphanes), and initiating the rebuilding of the temple.[24] But Herod's reign was murderous and megalomaniacal: he was not the king the Jews had been waiting for. According to his own angry caprice, Herod ordered the deaths of an uncle, his mother-in-law, and three of his sons. And though he loved Mariamne best of his ten wives, Herod eventually killed her too, when he suspected infidelity. As Eugene Peterson describes in *The Jesus Way*, even Caesar Augustus acknowledged Herod's unquenchable bloodthirst: "I would rather be Herod's pig than his son."[25]

It is little wonder, then, that we should see genocide on the first pages of Matthew's Gospel. Herod, murderously jealous of the infant King of the Jews, whom the wise men have traveled to worship, raises the sword of terror over Bethlehem. He orders the systematic murder of every little Bethlehemite boy, two years old and under, and dispenses (or so he thinks) of his rival. If Luke's Gospel rises on the anthems of the angels—"Glory to God in the highest, and on earth peace among those with whom he is pleased!"—Matthew's Gospel is carried in on voices of lament: Rachel weeps for her children and refuses to be comforted "because they are no more" (Mt 2:18). Jesus' birth is accompanied by the untimely, cruel death of innocent children at the hands of a political savage; his first home is no safe place.

Nor is it a permanent place. Joseph, having been warned about Herod by an angel, takes his wife and young son and flees by night to Egypt. The holy family, like the hundreds of thousands of refugees spilling out of Syria and flooding into Europe, take up home on their backs and become aliens in Egypt, which has long served in Israel's history as symbolic of slavery, not freedom. Like Naomi's family, Joseph and Mary and Jesus leave behind Bethlehem and make temporary home outside the borders of ancient Palestine. With their survival threatened, they choose to abandon all that is familiar and become cultural and linguistic strangers in a strange place.

The circumstances surrounding Jesus' birth remind the readers of Scripture that God entered a world dangerously familiar to our own, a world in which tyrants rule and innocents are slaughtered, a world bloated with injustice and gasping with fear, a world that cannot, according to all of our domestic instincts, be home. Thanks be to the enfleshed God, he is no stranger to our grief. He knows home as the handful of dirty sand slipping through our fingers and spilling at our feet.

GOD-FORSAKEN SON

The tumult and turmoil surrounding the birth narratives of Jesus do not describe the greatest grief of the one the prophet Isaiah called "Man of Sorrows." Jesus' worst alienation was not as a result of Herod's death warrant or his two-year exile in Egypt; it was the violent crucifixion he suffered at the hands of a cowardly Pilate, whose job it was to quell any threat of Jewish revolt. And lest we think that it was the crowds and Pilate who put the Son of God to death, we must hear Peter thunder from the pulpit at the very first Pentecost: "Jesus [was] delivered up to the definite plan and foreknowledge of God" (Acts 2:23). The innocent Son of God shouldered the guilt for the treachery committed in the Garden. He willed to be forsaken that we might be taken in.

Psalm 22, written many centuries before the birth and death of Jesus Christ, makes haunting prediction of his suffering at the hands of the Romans: his hands and his feet would be pierced; they would gamble for his clothing; he would cry out in desperate, agonizing thirst. As Charles Spurgeon suggests, it is possible that Jesus recited the entirety of this psalm—from "My God, my God, why have you forsaken me?" to "He has done it"—while he hoisted himself up and heaved for breath.

The psalmist describes not just the physical suffering that reduces his body to a bag of bones, his heart to melted wax, but the spiritual suffering endured because of God's silence. Despite cries of anguish, God stands at a remove from the sufferer—because the wages of sin must be paid by death. And though Psalm 22 writhes with anguish, it also affirms steadfast hope in Israel's God of deliverance. With every labored breath Jesus might have recalled the history of God's faithfulness. Maybe he remembers the ten fateful plagues, the rescue at the banks of the Red Sea, water from the rock, bread from heaven, and military victory achieved by trumpet blast. Maybe he also recalls the day an angel of the Lord stood with unsheathed sword over Jerusalem after King David had ordered the census of the national population against divine prohibition and God commanded punishment for his sin.

First Chronicles 21 records that David was given his choice of divine poison: either three years of famine, three months of military defeat, or three days of divine scourge. "Let me fall into the hand of the LORD, for his mercy is very great," David eventually decides. But when the angel arrives at Jerusalem, God stays his hand, as David seems to almost expect, and it's on the site of this mercy, on the threshing floor of Ornan, that David promises to build the temple. Israel's home of worship will commemorate the God who relents. From the cross Jesus might have recalled the day a sword was mercifully sheathed in Jerusalem, the sword that centuries later fell with judgment at Golgotha.

We should not wonder that the sparrow and swallow of Psalm 84 find their home at the altar of God. The promise of pardon is their invitation of welcome.

> How lovely is your dwelling place,
>   O LORD of hosts!
> My soul longs, yes, faints
>   for the courts of the LORD;
> my heart and flesh sing for joy
>   to the living God.
> Even the sparrow finds a home
>   and the swallow a nest for herself,
>   where she may lay her young,
> at your altars, O LORD of hosts,
>   my King and my God.
> Blessed are those who dwell in your house,
>   ever singing your praise! (Psalm 84:1-4)

Like them, we are looking for a place to roost.

According to eyewitness accounts and the evidence of an empty tomb, Jesus of Nazareth died—and then, three days later, left behind his grave clothes, appearing to hundreds of his followers. He rose from the dead, inaugurating, as N. T. Wright puts it, "God's new creation right in the middle of the old one."[26] He defeated death and delivered God's people from the perished things. His resurrected body is now proof that his church will be brought forward to the new earth, pictured in Revelation 21 as the city of God coming down out of heaven like a bejeweled bride on her wedding day. "Behold, the dwelling place of God is with man. He will dwell with them, and they will be his people, and God himself will be with them as their God. He will wipe away every tear from their eyes, and death shall be no more, neither shall there be mourning, nor crying, nor pain anymore, for the former things have passed away" (vv. 3-4). Homelessness ends in the new Jerusalem, where God keeps place for his people. By the light of the Lamb, home is made luminous, and it is a light to banish gloom and darkness, death and despair.

Behold, God says. I am making all things new.

151 GLENDON AVENUE
TORONTO, ONTARIO

I RETURN FROM CARING FOR MY MOTHER on a Saturday, and as seems fitting, the seven of us report to the American consulate in Toronto on Monday to renew our passports. A week later, I go back to pick them up and am greeted by another American expatriate in the elevator. "You're not here to give up your citizenship, are you?" No, I reassure, hearing him exhale relief. Three weeks later, Ryan is offered a promotion, which allows us, for the foreseeable future, the luxury of staying put. There is nothing certain, of course, about our future, but I am less anxious about that uncertainty. I may have no permanent home in Toronto, but I have the housekeeping. And aren't we all waiting on home?

The ancient Israelites were commanded to recite a liturgy when they entered the land of promise and offered to God the gifts of their first harvest. I imagine taking it up in chorus as we enter the gates of the new Jerusalem—the moment homelessness and all of its attendant grief will be laid to rest:

> A wandering Aramean was my father.
> He went down into Egypt and sojourned there, and the
>   Egyptians treated us harshly.
> But the Lord brought us out of Egypt with a mighty
>   hand.
> He brought us into this land, which flows with milk and
>   honey.

This is a song to make sense of life's lament and longing, peril and promise. And it's the song we'll be singing when we fall into the sojourning, suffering arms of Jesus.

I declare today that I am finally home.

ACKNOWLEDGMENTS

IF YOUR PARENTS ARE STILL ALIVE, call them today and ask them to describe the day you were born," Amy Poehler advises in her memoir, *Yes Please*. I'm not really given to that impulse. Aside from knowing that I was born at 3:01 a.m. and was the "best gift" my mother ever received on Mother's Day, I know little of the event. But I have other stories. Having birthed five children, I can turn a tale.

I am happy to share in the pages of *Keeping Place* some of the stories from my family. But I have written them not simply for the purposes of this book; I have written them as memory to bequeath. As an undergraduate at Wheaton College I used to imagine marrying a man I could be comfortable enough with to sing at the top of my lungs. By that standard and many more, Ryan, you have been God's gift to me. To my oldest daughter, Audrey, who is not only an emerging writer and musician, but a lovely young woman of God: one of my cherished memories will be our trip to Rwanda with Hope International in 2015, even our final panic when we were denied boarding on our return flight. To my oldest son, Nathan: every day I marvel at your tenderness and playful patience with your younger brothers. Our home is a better place with you in it. Please consider this a kiss that you can't wipe off. To Camille, our youngest daughter: I am proud of the young woman you're becoming, especially your hard work of loving those on the margins. And by the way, I'm also grateful for your dedicated housekeeping. To Andrew, the oldest of the twins: I see you growing in your love for stories, most of all your love for God's Word. I pray you'll spend the rest of your life reading with wide eyes. To Colin, the tallest of the twins: I won't forget that you're the only person in the family who cried when Tony got down on his knees to confess to his wife in the movie *War Room*. You are a deeply sensitive boy, and I pray you will always work for God's good pleasure.

Professionally, I couldn't do this work apart from a team of friends. From IVP: Jeff Crosby, your enthusiasm for my work diminishes self-doubt. Cindy Bunch: thank you for the pointed yet gentle criticism of my muddled first draft. There are many more people to thank at IVP, but let me just say that it is my great privilege to continue this publishing partnership. I'm also grateful to belong to several groups of writers who are committed to sharing their collective expertise and encouragement: the regular contributors to *Christianity Today*, Redbud Writers Guild, Ink Creative Collective, and OKJFC. Specifically, I'm indebted to Dorothy Greco, an early reader of this book, as well as Aleah Marsden and Bronwyn Lea, who I pray with regularly on (early!) morning conference calls. As well, Bethany Jenkins, editor at The Gospel Coalition, was an early supporter of *Teach Us to Want* and has since become a treasured friend. Additionally, I am grateful for Beth Booram, whose spiritual direction has been an answer to prayer. Finally, I would be remiss to not also thank Scott Sauls for offering such an apt foreword for this book.

Most of all, thank you staff, and members of Grace Toronto Church: I believe we, however feebly, have taken up part of Toronto's housekeeping. May Christ be known and praised.

STUDY GUIDE

Session 1

VIDEO CONTENT

1. Describe a home where you've felt warmly welcomed. What made that particular home feel so inviting?

2. Read Genesis 1–2. Where do you see evidence of God's homemaking in these chapters?

3. If it's true that home requires connection to place, connection to one another, and connection to God, how does this change your perspective, even your pursuit of home? What happens if one of those three elements is missing?

4. "There's no place like home." According to Genesis 3, why is this tragically true? What is the inevitable outcome of expecting to have a perfect home here and now?

BOOK CONTENT

Chapter 1: Nostalgia

1. Describe an experience of homesickness. Why did you feel far from home?

2. Where's home for you? Talk about the place(s) you most identify as home.

3. Have you ever thought of the Bible's redemptive narrative as the story of home? How does that perspective shape or alter the way you view God's dramatic work of salvation?

Chapter 2: Angel in the House

1. What cultural assumptions do you bring to a book about home? Did you grow up in a home where gender roles were strictly defined?

2. Why is a historical understanding of home important for the task of biblical study? What missteps are possible if we neglect it?

3. Which of the domestic images of God resonated most with you? How does that image enrich your view of God?

Chapter 3: Taken In

1. What care is necessary for a home to feel like home? Who has cared for you in that way? Or whose neglect or abuse communicated lack of care?

2. How does the image of God as homemaker enrich your view of him? How does it inform the way you view the work of homemaking?

Session 2

VIDEO CONTENT

1. Have you ever felt a deep connection to place? Do you have it now? Why or why not?

2. Read Genesis 28:10-22, Genesis 31, and Genesis 32. Consider how Jacob met God in these three "in-between" places (Bethel, Gilead, and Jabbok). In your own life, where have you met God unexpectedly—in "in-between" places?

3. According to Scripture, Jesus was the God who "tabernacled" in our midst (Jn 1:14); it's in God that we "live and move and have our being" (Acts 17:28); and we serve a God who will

"never leave or forsake us" (Heb 13:5). What comfort does this traveling, tabernacling, indwelling God give you for your present circumstances?

4. Read Ruth 1. Has there been a time in your life when you've felt like Naomi—that life was "bitter," that God gave you emptiness rather than fullness? How did you take refuge in God as Ruth did? Or how might circumstances have been different if you had?

BOOK CONTENT

Chapter 4: Border Crossings

1. How connected do you feel to the place you currently live? What contributes to your relative sense of belonging or dislocation?

2. If you told your faith story as a story of *place*, where would you begin, and where would you end up? How do each of these places testify to God's sovereign care in your life?

3. What evidence of restlessness can you identify in your life? What invitation to stability might you receive?

4. How does Jacob's story encourage you to trust the God of the liminal places? How could you live your own "in-betweens" differently?

Chapter 5: Perished Things

1. What experiences have taught you about the fragility of life? Describe how life's fragility inspires either fear or faith.

2. What should we assume about the God who takes such deliberate care of the widow? Practically, how does understanding God's care of the widow encourage you in your needs and quiet anxieties?

3. What answer does the gospel give to the perished things? Is this a hope you feel confident to share with people outside your faith community?

4. In what ways are you tempted to confide your hope in an earthly home and family? What might it look like to receive these as good gifts while yet recognizing them as temporal?

Session 3

VIDEO CONTENT

1. Read the parable of the prodigal son in Luke 15:11-32. Now imagine yourself not as one of the sons but as the father. What new insights from this familiar story do you gain regarding your role and responsibilities in God's kingdom?

2. Read the three stories of Joseph mentioned in this session's first teaching segment (Gen 39–41). How is Joseph's housekeeping a blessing to Potiphar and the prison warden as well as Pharaoh and the kingdom of Egypt? How might this be a fulfillment of the gospel promise God gave to Abraham in Genesis 12:1-3?

3. If you're honest with yourself, do you think of relationships within your church as being as primary as your family relationships? What makes it easy to treat relationships within church as temporary? (Think, for example, of the term "church shopping.")

4. If the church is home and family, we should probably expect as many disappointments as the ones we have had in our childhood homes and with our biological families. Read

ahead in Joseph's story (especially Gen 45:1–15) to understand what forgiveness practically looks like. How does his
story inspire your willingness to forgive your brothers and
sisters in Christ?

BOOK CONTENT

Chapter 6: A Suffering Servant

1. Can you give examples of occasions or seasons when the
practice of love has felt like "intimate drudgery"?

2. Consider the dual actions of God's love: that it blesses *and*
sends. Which are you tempted to give more weight to? Why
are both necessary to the gospel?

3. Can you identify temptations you face in wanting the *benefits*
of home without the *burdens* of the housekeeping?

4. How do the stories of Joseph and Jesus inform an understanding of your personal call to the housekeeping? Who is
God calling you to serve, and how?

Chapter 7: House of God

1. While there is no exact parallel between ancient Israel's tab-
ernacle/temple and the New Testament church, what can we
learn from Israel's worship practices? How might this inform
our understanding and experience of church?

2. What might we have to give up, individually and corporately,
in order to right-size the church's importance? What do we
stand to gain if church becomes bigger (and the nuclear
family smaller)?

3. How can your local church begin to take more seriously its
call to the housekeeping of its neighborhood? What practices
will be needed to overcome insularity?

Session 4

VIDEO CONTENT

1. How do your own expectations for marriage differ from what we learn in Scripture—that marriage is a picture of the love relationship between Christ and his church (reread Eph 5:22-33)? How are those expectations affecting either your dating relationships or your marriage?

2. If you're willing to share, what longings for marriage do you have (if you're single)? What disappointments of marriage do you have (if you're married)? What would change if you began to believe that marriage was meant as an embodied gospel witness to the world?

3. Do you have the habit of inviting others into your home? What's one excuse you'd have to stop making in order for hospitality to become your regular habit?

4. Consider that the meals of Scripture were a means for formation, proclamation, and justice. Read 1 Corinthians 11:17-34 and note each of these elements present in the Lord's Supper. Which element hadn't you considered before? What will change about your practice of "feast keeping" as you incorporate that element?

BOOK CONTENT

Chapter 8: Love and Marriage

1. What expectations of marriage have we imported from culture? Which of these have we baptized as biblical? To what detriment?

2. For what purpose might the Holy Spirit have inspired the record of David's fraught family life? Why might the stories

of women like Michal, Abigail, and Bathsheba be included in the canon?

3. If you are married, what are the challenges of having and holding your spouse in your particular season? If you are unmarried, what are the challenges of living without a spouse in your particular season?

4. How can the church affirm the goodness of marriage and family without making these ultimate measures of the good life?

Chapter 9: Saying Grace

1. North American culture is beleaguered in its relationship to food. What contributes to our inability to regard food in healthy, holy ways?

2. Describe some of the food and feast experiences you've shared with God's people. Have you been the beneficiary of someone's hospitality? Do you like to play host? Does your church extend regular invitations for communal eating?

3. Like Israel, could you be accused of the "failure to feast"? What are the spiritual consequences of your neglect? How can you recover feasting as a spiritual practice?

4. How might you (and your church) more readily long for the hungry to be fed? Together, how might you become more committed in practice to feeding the hungry?

Session 5

VIDEO CONTENT

1. What are the ways you usually try to deal with your busyness and exhaustion? Does it satisfy your deep longing for rest? Why or why not?

2. Read the Old Testament sabbath passages Exodus 20:8-11 and Deuteronomy 5:12-15. What do these passages teach you about God? About humanity? About work and about rest?

3. The Biblical story begins and ends at home. Read Revelation 21. What aspect of your final, eternal home in the new Jerusalem is most comforting to you? Most surprising?

4. If the story of the Bible is the story of home—and the longing for home is our deepest human desire—consider who you might share this story with. What friend, family member, neighbor, or colleague would be deeply consoled to know that there is a homemaking God who sent us his Son to rescue us, his homesick people?

BOOK CONTENT

Chapter 10: Cathedral in Time

1. Without the regular practice of rest, how does our commitment to the housekeeping become corrupt?

2. Describe how our culture imposes "burdens" on us, much like ancient Egypt drove Israel mercilessly hard. Why is resistance so difficult?

3. What were the Israelites taught to remember as they practiced sabbath? Why is holy memory so important for the practice of rest?

4. How do Christians understand and practice sabbath differently than Jews?

Chapter 11: City of God

1. If home calls us to our most proximal obligations, which "neighbor" is God calling you to love? What forgiveness might be required to love them well? What humble service?

2. What do our experiences of displacement and despair teach us about home? How can grief be a surprising source of encouragement?

3. Why is it necessary, in the story of home, to talk about exclusion as well as embrace? Does the idea of God's exclusion chafe? Why?

4. How does Jesus' alienation and God-forsakenness help you make sense of your disappointments with home?

5. Begin to imagine how you might script your own homecoming song as you enter the New Jerusalem—and fall into the "sojourning, suffering arms of Jesus." What song will be on your lips?

NOTES

PREFACE

[1]Frederick Buechner, *The Longing for Home* (New York: HarperCollins, 1996), Kindle ed., chap. 1.

[2]Wendell Berry, *Jayber Crow* (Berkeley, CA: Counterpoint, 2000).

[3]Charles Marsh and John Perkins, *Welcoming Justice* (Downers Grove, IL: InterVarsity Press, 2009), Kindle ed., chap. 4.

[4]Julian Barnes, quoted in James K. A. Smith, *How (Not) to Be Secular* (Grand Rapids: Eerdmans, 2014), 5.

[5]Glenna Matthews, *Just a Housewife* (New York: Oxford University Press, 1987), Kindle ed., chap. 3.

[6]Ibid., chap. 1.

[7]Smith, *How (Not) to Be Secular,* 25.

1 NOSTALGIA: THE LONGING FOR HOME

[1]Gracie Lofthouse, "How Language Influences Emotion," *Atlantic*, December 17, 2015, www.theatlantic.com/health/archive/2015/12/the-book-of-human-emotions-language-feelings/420978.

[2]Curiously, in the Latin or Slavic European languages, there is no equivalent to the word *home*. The French, for example, have a word for house (*maison*) and an expression for home in terms of location (*chez soi*), but the latter lacks the emotional dimensions of the English word *home*. In France, one can return *chez soi*, but only in sense of physical displacement—a linguistic difference, which points to varying cultural sensibilities of home. Witold Rybczynski discusses these linguistic differences in his book *Home: A Short History of an Idea* (New York: Penguin, 1986), 62.

[3]Homer, *The Odyssey* bk. 1, lines 217-18, trans. Richard Lattimore (New York: HarperCollins, 1967), Kindle ed.

[4]Julian Barnes, quoted in James K. A. Smith, *How (Not) to be Secular* (Grand Rapids: Eerdmans, 2014), 4.

[5]Georg Lukács, quoted in James Wood, "On Not Going Home," *London Review of Books*, February 20, 2014, www.lrb.co.uk/v36/n04/james-wood /on-not-going-home.

[6]Marilynne Robinson, *Lila* (New York: Farrar, Straus & Giroux, 2014), 5.

[7]Ibid., 258.

[8]On Tuesday, January 26, 2016, the Danish parliament voted to seize refugees' assets to cover the cost of their asylum.

[9]Warsan Shire, "Home," in *SeekersHub*, September 2, 2015, www.seekershub .org/blog/2015/09/home-warsan-shire.

[10]Craig G. Bartholomew, *Where Mortals Dwell* (Grand Rapids: Baker Academic, 2011), xi.

[11]Ibid., 30.

[12]Ellen Davis, *Getting Involved with God* (Cambridge, MA: Cowley, 2001), 55.

[13]Albert Camus, *The Myth of Sisyphus* (New York: Penguin, 1975), 13.

[14]Ibid., 13.

[15]Ibid., 53.

[16]Philip Zaleski and Carol Zaleski, *The Fellowship: The Literary Lives of the Inklings* (New York: Farrar, Straus & Giroux, 2015), 246.

[17]Ibid., 511.

[18]Ibid.

2 ANGEL IN THE HOUSE: A BRIEF HISTORY

[1]Phyllis Rose, *Parallel Lives* (New York: Alfred A. Knopf, 1984), 6.

[2]Ruth Padel, *52 Ways of Looking at a Poem* (London: Vintage Books, 2004), 43.

[3]Witold Rybczynski, *Home: A Short History of an Idea* (New York: Penguin, 1986), 71.

[4]As Rybczynski discusses, in the Middle Ages only the middle class had anything comparable to what we might now call a "home." The aristocrats lived in castles, and the clerics lived in monasteries. The serfs lived in hovels, which hardly resembled homes (ibid., 24–36).

[5]Ibid., 70.

[6]Nancy Pearcey, *Total Truth* (Wheaton, IL: Crossway, 2004), 327.

[7]Carolyn McCulley with Nora Shank, *The Measure of Success* (Nashville: B&H, 2014), Kindle ed., chap. 3.

[8]Ibid.

[9]Ibid.

[10]Ibid.

[11]Glenna Matthews, *Just a Housewife* (New York: Oxford University Press, 1987), Kindle ed., chap. 1.

[12]Ibid.

[13]Ibid., chap. 4.

[14]Ibid., chap. 5.

[15]Robert and Helen Lynd's *Middletown* (New York: Harcourt Brace & Jovanovich, 1959) demonstrates just how radical was the transformation between 1890 and 1925.

[16]Gail Collins, *When Everything Changed* (New York: Hachette, 2009), 53.

[17]New technologies like frozen and processed food deskilled the cooking process and ushered in the "cream-of-mushroom-soup school of cuisine" in the 1950s. As an example, green bean casserole, a traditional Thanksgiving dish served to many American families, was a recipe created by home economist Dorcas Reilly in 1955.

[18]Matthews, *Just a Housewife*, chap. 8.

[19]Ibid.

[20]Caitlin Flanagan, *To Hell with All That* (New York: Little, Brown, 2006), 174.

[21]This inevitable feeling of male intrusion into domestic spaces was painted by the Dutch. "When a male is included in a Vermeer, one has the sense that he is a visitor—an intruder—for these women do not simply inhabit these rooms, they occupy them completely. Whether they are sewing, playing the spinet, or reading a letter, the Dutch women are solidly, emphatically, contentedly at home" (Rybczynski, *Home*, 71).

[22]Flanagan's book *To Hell with All That* is subtitled *Loving and Loathing Our Inner Housewife.*

[23]Coventry Patmore, "Angel in the House," 1854. This angel, writes Virginia Woolf, was "intensely sympathetic. She was immensely charming. She was utterly unselfish. She excelled in the difficult arts of family life. She sacrificed herself daily. If there was chicken, she took the leg; if there was a draught she sat in it—in short she was so constituted that she never had a mind or a wish of her own, but preferred to sympathize always with the minds and wishes of others." Virginia Woolf, quoted in Brigid Schulte, *Overwhelmed* (Toronto: HarperCollins, 2014), 190.

[24]Flanagan, *To Hell with All That*, 224-25.

[25]Ibid., xvii.

[26]Collins, *When Everything Changed*, 337.

[27]R. Kent Hughes and Bryan Chapell, *1–2 Timothy and Titus* (Wheaton, IL: Crossway, 2000), 330.

[28]Lauren Winner, *Wearing God* (New York: HarperOne, 2015), 138.

[29]Ibid., 139.

[30]Ibid., 138-39.

[31]Kenneth E. Bailey, *The Good Shepherd* (Downers Grove, IL: IVP Academic, 2014), 149.

[32]Ibid., 55.

3 TAKEN IN: THE FIRST MAKER OF HOME

[1]Sandra Tsing Loh, "The Weaker Sex," *Atlantic,* October 2012, www.the atlantic.com/magazine/archive/2012/10/the-weaker-sex/309094.

[2]Hanna Rosin, *The End of Men* (New York: Penguin Books, 2012).

[3]Tsing Loh, "Weaker Sex."

[4]Ibid.

[5]Cheryl Mendelson, *Home Comforts* (New York: Scribner, 1999), Kindle ed., chap. 1.

[6]Ibid.

[7]Ibid.

[8]Ibid., chap. 7.

[9]Ibid., chap. 1.

[10]John H. Sailhamer, *The Pentateuch as Narrative* (Grand Rapids: Zondervan, 1992), 88.

[11]Andy Crouch, *Culture Making* (Downers Grove, IL: InterVarsity Press, 2008), 103.

[12]Craig G. Bartholomew, *Where Mortals Dwell* (Grand Rapids: Baker Academic, 2011), 27.

[13]Sailhamer, *The Pentateuch as Narrative*, 100. Incidentally, the ESV does not always translate this Hebrew word as "put." Sometimes it is translated "set outside" or "give rest."

[14]Ibid., 100.

[15]Ibid., 101.

[16]David Leeming and Margaret Leeming, *A Dictionary of Creation Myths* (New York: Oxford University Press, 1995), 117.

[17]Ellen Davis, *Getting Involved with God* (Cambridge, MA: Cowley, 2001), 139.

[18]Ibid.

[19]C. S. Lewis, *Mere Christianity,* in *The Complete C. S. Lewis Signature Classics* (New York: HarperCollins, 2002), 46.

[20]Thomas C. Oden, *Life in the Spirit* (San Francisco: HarperCollins, 1992), 127.

[21]Ibid., 198.

4 BORDER CROSSINGS: ON (NOT) STAYING PUT

[1]"A Geotourism Hotspot: National Geographic," *Evergreen Brick Works*, February 16, 2016. www.evergreen.ca/blog/entry/a-geotourism-hotspot-national-geographic.

[2]Eric Jaffe, "Reclaiming the Public Square," *Atlantic*, July–August, 2015, www.theatlantic.com/magazine/archive/2015/07/reclaiming-the-public-square/395285.

[3]Kirk Johnson, "House That Wouldn't Budge (or Float Away) Faces a Last Stand," *New York Times,* April 11, 2015, www.nytimes.com/2015/04/12/us/house-that-wouldnt-budge-or-float-away-faces-a-last-stand.html?_r=0.

[4]Elahe Izadi, "The 'Up' House Is for Sale. Its Future Is in the Air," *Washington Post*, April 24, 2015, www.washingtonpost.com/news/morning-mix/wp/2015/04/24/the-up-house-is-for-sale-its-future-is-in-the-air.

[5]I first heard the history of technology formulated in this way by Dr. Read Schuchardt in a series of lectures delivered at College Church in Wheaton, Illinois, in 2008.

[6]John H. Sailhamer, *The Pentateuch as Narrative* (Grand Rapids: Zondervan, 1992), 141.

[7]Brad Plumer, "Americans Still Move Around More Than Anyone Else in the World," *Washington Post,* February 16, 2016, www.washingtonpost.com/news/wonk/wp/2013/05/15/the-united-states-is-still-one-of-the-most-mobile-countries-in-the-world.

[8]Walter Brueggemann, *The Land* (Philadelphia: Fortress, 1977), 3-4.

[9]James Wood, "On Not Going Home," *London Review of Books*, February 20, 2014, www.lrb.co.uk/v36/n04/james-wood/on-not-going-home.

[10]Jonathan Wilson-Hartgrove, *The Wisdom of Stability* (Brewster, MA: Paraclete, 2011), 2.

[11]Ibid.,179.

[12]Marilynne Robinson, "The Fate of Ideas: Moses," in *When I Was a Child I Read Books* (Toronto: HarperCollins, 2012), 105.

[13]To be clear, this home is not heaven, at least in the way we normally think of it. Heaven, as N. T. Wright describes in *Surprised by Hope*, is where God reigns presently. One day, the kingdom of heaven will descend to earth. "Heaven is the place where *God's purposes for the future are stored up*. It isn't where they are meant to stay so that one would need to go to heaven to enjoy them; it is where they are kept safe against the day when they will become a reality on

earth" (N. T. Wright, *Surprised by Hope* [New York: HarperCollins, 2009], 151). As the Lord's Prayer suggests and as John's Patmos vision insists, Christians will not ascend to heaven but heaven will descend to earth. Our future is not celestial but earthly; not disembodied but material.

[14]Robert Alter, *The Five Books of Moses* (New York: W. W. Norton, 2004), 149.

[15]Wilson-Hartgrove, *Wisdom of Stability*, 14-15.

[16]This is also part of Rebekah's ruse to save her favored son from the murderous hands of his twin brother, who he has stolen birthright and blessing from.

[17]Wilson-Hartgrove, *Wisdom of Stability*, 15.

[18]This translation of Genesis 31:42 comes from Alter, *Five Books of Moses*, 174.

[19]Ibid., 168.

[20]Ibid.

[21]Ibid., 177.

[22]Esther de Waal, *Seeking God* (Collegeville, MN: Liturgical Press, 1984), 64.

[23]Antony, quoted in Wilson-Hartgrove, *Wisdom of Stability*, 35.

5 PERISHED THINGS: AND IMPERISHABLE HOME

[1]David Brooks, "Going Home Again," *New York Times*, March 20, 2014, www .nytimes.com/2014/03/21/opinion/brooks-going-home-again.html?_r=0.

[2]Marilynne Robinson, *Housekeeping* (New York: Farrar, Straus & Giroux, 1980), 92.

[3]Nicholas Wolterstorff, *Lament for a Son* (Grand Rapids: Eerdmans, 1987), Kindle edition.

[4]Ibid.

[5]This seems to have been as much a sacrificial service to the dead as to the living.

[6]Carolyn Custis James, *The Gospel of Ruth* (Grand Rapids: Zondervan, 2008), Kindle ed., chap. 2.

[7]Ibid., chap. 4.

[8]Ibid., chap. 8.

[9]Ibid.

[10]Translation of Genesis 21:7 from Robert Alter, *The Five Books of Moses* (New York: W. W. Norton, 2004).

6 A SUFFERING SERVANT: THE LABOR OF LOVE

[1]Stephen Marche, "The Case for Filth," *New York Times*, December 7, 2013, www.nytimes.com/2013/12/08/opinion/sunday/the-case-for-filth.html.

[2]Ibid.

[3]Glenna Matthews, *Just a Housewife* (New York: Oxford University Press, 1987), Kindle ed., chap. 4.

[4]Read Mercer Schuchardt, "The Medium is the Messiah: McLuhan's Religion and its Relationship to His Media Theory," *Second Nature Journal*, April 1, 2013, http://secondnaturejournal.com/the-medium-is-the-messiah-mcluhans -religion-and-its-relationship-to-his-media-theory.

[5]Esther of Sylvia Plath's *The Bell Jar*, quoted in Kathleen Norris, *The Quotidian Mysteries* (New York: Paulist, 1998), Kindle.

[6]Roberto A. Ferdman, "The Baffling Reason Many Millennials Don't Eat Cereal," *Washington Post*, February 23, 2016, www.washingtonpost.com/news /wonk/wp/2016/02/23/this-is-the-height-of-laziness.

[7]Marilynne Robinson, "When I Was a Child," in *When I Was a Child I Read Books* (Toronto: HarperCollins, 2012), 93.

[8]Andy Crouch, *Playing God* (Downers Grove, IL: InterVarsity Press, 2013), 235.

[9]Ibid., 241.

[10]C. S. Lewis, *Mere Christianity*, in *The Complete C. S. Lewis Signature Classics* (New York: HarperCollins, 2002), 113.

[11]Simone de Beauvoir, quoted in Marche, "Case for Filth."

[12]Henri Nouwen, *The Return of the Prodigal Son* (New York: Doubleday, 1996), 5.

[13]Ibid., 122.

[14]Robert Alter, *The Five Books of Moses* (New York: W. W. Norton, 2004), 221.

[15]The Hebrew word *beyt sohar* emphasizes both *prison* and *house*.

[16]Alter, *Five Books of Moses*, 237.

[17]See Adam McHugh, *The Listening Life* (Downers Grove, IL: InterVarsity Press, 2015).

[18]Eugene Peterson, *The Jesus Way* (Grand Rapids: Eerdmans, 2007), 171.

[19]Ibid., 177.

[20]Ibid., 179.

7 HOUSE OF GOD: THE CHURCH AS HOME

[1]Eneri Taul, quoted in Joe O'Connor, "Toronto Church's Stained Glass Window Tells the Frightening Story of Another Refugee Influx—from Estonia," *National Post*, December 23, 2015.

[2]Ibid.

[3]Robert Alter, *The Five Books of Moses* (New York: W. W. Norton, 2004), 469.

[4]Ibid., 305.

[5]Alter writes, "The Hebrew construction . . . is unusual [for Exodus 35:22]. It would appear to suggest that the women queued up first to offer their donations. . . . Now we are alerted to the fact that women played an important role in the outpouring of contributions for the Tabernacle" (ibid., 516).

[6]John H. Sailhamer, *The Pentateuch as Narrative* (Grand Rapids: Zondervan, 1992), 298.

[7]John Walton, *The Lost World of Genesis One* (Downers Grove, IL: IVP Academic, 2009), 50.

[8]Ibid., 68.

[9]Ibid., 71.

[10]Augustine, *The Confessions* (New York: Oxford University Press, 1998), 145.

[11]Wesley Hill, *Spiritual Friendship* (Grand Rapids: Brazos Press, 2015), 39.

[12]Ibid., 41.

[13]James K. A. Smith, *Desiring the Kingdom* (Grand Rapids: Baker Academic, 2009), 186.

[14]Alexander Schmemann, *For the Life of the World*, in ibid., 186.

[15]Paul Sparks, Tim Soerens, and Dwight J. Friesen, *The New Parish* (Downers Grove, IL: InterVarsity Press, 2014), 57.

[16]C. Christopher Smith and John Pattison, *Slow Church* (Downers Grove, IL: InterVarsity Press, 2014), 73-74.

[17]Amy L. Sherman, *Kingdom Calling* (Downers Grove, IL: InterVarsity Press, 2011), 16.

[18]Ibid., 20.

8 LOVE AND MARRIAGE: THE ROUTINE WORK OF I DO

[1]C. S. Lewis, *Mere Christianity*, in *The Complete C. S. Lewis Signature Classics* (New York: HarperCollins, 2002), 94.

[2]G. K. Chesterton, *Orthodoxy* (Peabody, MA: Hendrickson, 1908), 55.

[3]Caitlin Flanagan has a fascinating chapter on the housekeeping of marital sex in her book *To Hell with All That*. She writes, "Once children come along, it's easy for parents to regard each other as copresidents of an industrious little corporatation. . . . But the element that regularly restores a marriage to something with an aspect of romance rather than collegiality is sex."

[4]Gustave Flaubert, *Madame Bovary* (New York: Penguin, 1992), 271.

[5]Ibid., 116-17.

[6]Andrew L. Yarrow, "Falling Marriage Rates Reveal Economic Fault Lines," *New York Times*, February 6, 2015.

[7]James K. A. Smith, *How (Not) to Be Secular* (Grand Rapids: Eerdmans, 2014), 32.

[8]Ibid., 37.

[9]George Eliot, quoted in Phyllis Rose, *Parallel Lives* (New York: Alfred A. Knopf, 1984), 219.

[10]This is Phyllis Rose's observation based on the life and career of Charles Dickens. "Why is it today, when ambitious young women who have postponed marriage in order to launch their careers finally look around for someone to marry, so few men seem to be available? Perhaps because ambitious men marry young. Marriage and career, family and work, which so often pull a woman in different directions, are much more likely to reinforce one another for a man. Dickens provides a good case in point. Professionally, his marriage helped him. His household was arranged for him. . . . Not only was he working for his own advantage and to satisfy his own ambition, he was working for her, for them, for their children. The guilt a woman artist might feel in removing herself from her family in order to create is less likely to trouble a man, a man who imagines himself—as Dickens did—working *for* his family" (ibid., 150-51).

[11]Hanna Rosin, *The End of Men* (New York: Riverhead, 2012), 21.

[12]Ibid., 35.

[13]Courtney Hodell, "Babes in the Woods," in *Selfish, Shallow, and Self-Absorbed*, ed. Meghan Daum (New York: Picador, 2015).

[14]Laura Kipnis, "Maternal Instincts," in Daum, *Selfish, Shallow, and Self-Absorbed*.

[15]Wendell Berry, "Feminism, the Body, and the Machine," in *The Art of the Commonplace: The Agrarian Essays* (Washington, DC: Counterpoint, 2002), 66.

[16]Ibid., 67.

[17]Ibid., 71.

[18]N. T. Wright, *Scripture and the Authority of God* (New York: HarperCollins, 2011), Kindle ed., chap. 10.

[19]In 1 Samuel 26:44, Michal's second husband is called Palti. In 2 Samuel 3:15, he is referred to as Paltiel, although he is clearly the same man.

[20]Scot McKnight, "Worst-Great Book of the Year," *Jesus Creed* (blog), March 2, 2016, www.patheos.com/blogs/jesuscreed/2016/03/02/worst-great-book-of-the-year.

[21]Mark Spansel, "How to Combat Domestic Violence in the Church," *The Gospel Coalition* (blog), January 5, 2016, www.thegospelcoalition.org/article/how-to-combat-domestic-violence-in-the-church.

[22]Lewis, *Mere Christianity*, 91.

[23]Laura Merzig Fabrycky, "Genesis 15," in *Give Me the Word: Advent and Other Poems, 2000-2015* (Annandale: Saar River Press, 2015), 48.

9 SAYING GRACE: FEASTING TOGETHER

[1]Don Freeman, *Corduroy* (New York: Viking, 1968), 7.

[2]Ibid., 30.

[3]Jack Schwefel, quoted in Megan McArdle, "The Joy of Not Cooking," *Atlantic*, May 2011.

[4]Rachel Marie Stone, *Eat with Joy* (Downers Grove, IL: InterVarsity Press, 2013), Kindle ed., chap. 4.

[5]Ibid.

[6]Andrew B. McGowan, *Ancient Christian Worship* (Grand Rapids: Baker Academic, 2014), 19-20.

[7]Justin Martyr, quoted in ibid., 8.

[8]As McGowan mentions, other foods might also have been served such as fish, salt, vegetables, legumes, oil, and cheese (*Ancient Christian Worship*, 42).

[9]Tertullian, quoted in ibid., 22.

[10]McGowan, *Ancient Christian Worship*, 26.

[11]William T. Cavanaugh, *Being Consumed* (Grand Rapids: Eerdmans, 2008), Kindle ed., chap. 4.

[12]Nicaraguan Prayer, cited in Stone, *Eat With Joy*, chap. 2.

[13]Fannie Lou Hamer, quoted in Charles Marsh and John Perkins, *Welcoming Justice* (Downers Grove, IL: InterVarsity Press, 2009), Kindle ed., chap. 3.

10 CATHEDRAL IN TIME: A PLACE CALLED REST

[1]Gordon MacDonald, *Ordering Your Private World* (Nashville: Thomas Nelson, 2003), Kindle ed., chap. 14.

[2]Judith Shulevitz, *The Sabbath World: Glimpses of a Different Order of Time* (New York: Random House, 2010), Kindle ed., intro.

[3]Ibid.

[4]Josef Pieper, *Leisure: The Basis of Culture* (South Bend: St. Augustine's Press, 1998), 72.

[5]Andy Crouch, *Playing God* (Downers Grove, IL: InterVarsity Press, 2013), 252.

[6]Shulevitz, *Sabbath World*, pt. 5.

[7]Ibid., intro.

[8]Alice Morse Earle, quoted in ibid., pt. 5.

[9]Shulevitz, *Sabbath World*, pt. 5.

[10]N. T. Wright, *Scripture and the Authority of God* (New York: HarperCollins, 2011), Kindle ed., chap. 9.

[11]Ibid.

[12]Exodus 31:17 says, "On the seventh day, he rested and *was refreshed*." The Hebrew word for "refreshed" more literally means "to take breath."

[13]Pieper, "Leisure," intro.

[14]Ibid.

[15]Ibid., 50.

[16]Luci Shaw, "Still Life," in *Scape* (Eugene, OR: Cascade, 2013), 12.

11 CITY OF GOD: FINALLY HOME

[1]Jonathan Wilson-Hartgrove, *The Wisdom of Stability* (Brewster, MA: Paraclete, 2011), 112.

[2]Esther de Waal, *Seeking God* (Collegeville, MN: Liturgical Press, 2001), 57.

[3]Edith Schaeffer, *What Is a Family?* (Grand Rapids: Baker, 1975), Kindle ed., chap. 4.

[4]Ta-Nehisi Coates, "The Case for Reparations," *Atlantic*, June, 2014.

[5]Ibid.

[6]Ibid.

[7]Timothy Keller, *The Prodigal God* (New York: Dutton, 2008), 95.

[8]C. S. Lewis, *The Weight of Glory* (New York: HarperCollins, 1980), 42.

[9]"End the Gun Epidemic in America," *New York Times,* December 4, 2015, www.nytimes.com/2015/12/05/opinion/end-the-gun-epidemic-in-america.html.

[10]C. S. Lewis, *Mere Christianity*, in *The Complete C. S. Lewis Signature Classics* (New York: HarperCollins, 2002), 113.

[11]Ibid.

[12]Ibid.

[13]Ibid., 114.

[14]I have recently enjoyed reading N. T. Wright's *Surprised by Hope*. Although I haven't read Randy Alcorn's book *Heaven*, I know many have appreciated his thorough explanation of our embodied eternity with God.

[15]N. T. Wright, *Surprised by Hope* (New York: HarperCollins, 2009), Kindle ed., pref.

[16]Lewis, *Mere Christianity*, 112.

[17] In the Stanford marshmallow experiment, children who delayed gratification had better life outcomes, including educational achievement and physical health. In the Christian life, those who delay gratification for home have greater holiness and hope.

[18] C. S. Lewis, *The Weight of Glory: And Other Addresses* (New York: Harper-Collins, 2001), 31.

[19] G. K. Chesterton, "The House of Christmas," 1912.

[20] C. S. Lewis, *The Great Divorce,* in *The Complete C. S. Lewis Signature Classics* (New York: HarperCollins, 2002), 506.

[21] As I hope has been clear throughout the book, the righteousness of which I'm speaking here is not our righteous acts but those of Jesus Christ, who substituted his innocence for our guilt. "For our sake [God] made him [Jesus] to be sin who knew no sin, so that in him we might become the *righteousness of God*" (2 Cor 5:21).

[22] Wright, *Surprised by Hope*, chap. 11.

[23] James Wood, "On Not Going Home," *London Review of Books*, February 20, 2014, www.lrb.co.uk/v36/n04/james-wood/on-not-going-home.

[24] N. T. Wright, *The New Testament and the People of God* (Minneapolis: Fortress, 1992), 158-60.

[25] Eugene Peterson, *The Jesus Way* (Grand Rapids: Eerdmans, 2007), 201.

[26] Wright, *Surprised by Hope*, chap. 4.

ALSO BY
JEN POLLOCK MICHEL

Teach Us to Want
978-0-8308-4312-1

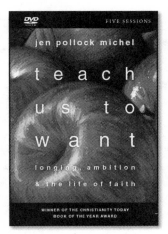

Teach Us to Want DVD
978-0-8308-4327-5

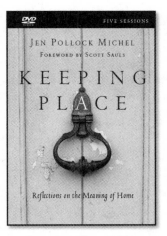

Keeping Place DVD
978-0-8308-4502-6